DALLAS
classic
DESSERTS

DALLAS *classic* DESSERTS

Recipes from Favorite Restaurants

HELEN THOMPSON

Foreword by Patricia Sharpe

Photography by Robert M. Peacock

PELICAN PUBLISHING COMPANY
Gretna 2009

The word "Pelican" and the depiction of a pelican are trademarks
of Pelican Publishing Company, Inc., and are registered in the
U.S. Patent and Trademark Office.
ISBN-13: 978-1-58980-624-5

Edited by Anne Michele Williams, Betsey Brairton,
Sara LaVere, and Andrea Chesman
Production by Angela Rojas
*Thanks to Casa Mexicana and to Cavender's Boot City
for permission to photograph*

Layout based on a design by Kit Wohl

Printed in China

Published by Pelican Publishing Company, Inc.
1000 Burmaster Street, Gretna, Louisiana 70053

Contents

Chapter 4   COBBLERS & CRISPS

Chapter 5   COOKIES, CANDIES & SUCH

Chapter 6   ICE CREAM & SAUCES

FOREWORD

When it comes to desserts, modern Dallas is an international city. Within its boundaries, one can eat flan and tres leches cake from Mexico, baklava from Greece, roasted bananas with tapioca and coconut milk from Vietnam, tiramisù from Italy, red rice with sweet red sesame paste from China, and pecan pie from Texas. The chefs may have learned from their mothers in the old country or graduated with distinction from the Culinary Institute of America. Their recipes may have been handed down for generations or created the night before.

But Dallas was not always a global melting pot. In its heart of hearts, it's a Southern town, and has been since its founding in 1841. Dallas is, after all, just 150 miles from Arkansas or Louisiana, and cotton was king in Texas as surely as it was in the rest of Dixie. The city's traditional desserts are staples of Southern comfort food: bread pudding, peach cobbler, lemon meringue pie, strawberry shortcake.

Once small, now large; once cohesive, now diverse; once provincial, now sophisticated, Dallas has grown up. Of course, change happens. Every Texas city is more refined now than when it started, but in Dallas, the level of cultural and culinary sophistication heightened quite quickly due to a mid-century boost from a powerful force: Neiman Marcus.

That a ladies' haute couture department store would be a force in the culinary world might seem far-fetched to those unaware of the extent of Neiman's influence. But not only was Neiman's the unquestioned style-setter in the South and Southwest, it was also within the city a destination for fine dining, thanks to a remarkable woman chef named Helen Corbitt.

Hired by Neiman's in 1955, the witty, strong-willed Corbitt taught Dallas about haute cuisine, both savory and sweet, for nearly fifteen years. Of course, she made the old-fashioned, homey desserts, but she also introduced caramel soufflés with English custard sauce, pears poached in white wine, cherries jubilee tipsy with brandy and kirsch, and buttermilk sherbet with avocado purée (how avant garde) to diners at the in-store Zodiac Room. Her signature creation was the Flowerpot, an individual Baked Alaska served in a crisp new clay flowerpot with a daisy poking through the meringue.

Corbitt's tables at the Zodiac were among the most urbane in town, and she reached people far beyond the ladies who lunch. Her diners were also business executives and members of the social-charitable-cultural cabal. She cooked, she taught sold-out classes, she wrote cookbooks. What Julia Child did for America, Helen Corbitt did for Dallas, and she started half a decade before the doyenne of French cooking published her first book.

Nearly four decades have passed since Corbitt's reign, and some of her dishes inevitably seem dated—nobody would serve Flowerpots except at a bridal shower. But her legacy of creativity and sophistication is very much alive, carried on by the Dallas chefs who came after her, whether they realize it or not. The whisk has passed to a new generation that both embraces the city's Southern roots and celebrates its multicultural present. Helen Corbitt was the bridge between those two extremes. She would no doubt be pleased.

—Patricia Sharpe
Executive Editor / Food Writer, Texas Monthly

INTRODUCTION

There is that old saying, "You can't have your cake and eat it, too." But when I was researching desserts for this book, I felt that I did have my cake and could—in fact, was required to—eat it, too. For an inveterate dessert-lover like me, that's the ideal situation to be in. I am that person who looks at the dessert side of the menu first, or who chooses a restaurant because they have a delicious Pavlova or chocolate cannolli. In fact, I have been known to order—and then, to eat—two desserts.

Research for this book involved several steps, the first of which was to narrow down among Dallas' many fine restaurants the many recipes we ended up featuring here. And from that list, we zeroed in on the desserts that are the classics of both the restaurant and also of the city. These are the desserts, among them Mint's green tea cake or Dean Fearing's glazed apple fritters, that have become iconic. And being iconic in a city full of icons—Peggy Sue BBQ, Craft and the Pyramid Grill, to name a few—is a very big deal.

I knew it already, but when I started writing about the restaurants it was almost overwhelming how many really great restaurants and chefs reside in Dallas. Major chefs, too, who have changed the course of culinary history. I'm talking specifically about Dean Fearing and Stephan Pyles, who—along with Houston chef Robert del Grande—dreamed up Southwestern cuisine a quarter of a century ago. These iconoclasts made the most of a fresh re-consideration of a genre of food that had descended into the hackneyed. Treated with the same respect and ingenuity that French chefs lavish on their creations, Tex-Mex quickly became couture. We all started thinking of food in a different way.

The National Restaurant Association has named Dallas the U.S. city with the most restaurants per capita. That could be both a blessing and a curse—just because a city has a lot of restaurants is no guarantee that the restaurants are good. It turns out, though, that Dallas has a robust penchant for dining out, and for dining out well. Many of its great restaurants are in hotels—the fabulously opulent hotels that reflect the city's stereotype of grand style. With that kind of gold standard being the norm, other restaurants simply have to measure up.

This book would not have been possible without the extravagant generosity of the city's great chefs and pastry chefs. They have bigheartedly given us the recipes for their best desserts, which we now share with you. These recipes are the result of long hours of thought, trial, error and triumph, and I am grateful to all the chefs and restaurant owners who happily participated in this project. Home cooks who read this book will know what it means to give away one's secrets of the trade. My hope and expectation is that readers of this book will enjoy being in on them.

—Helen Thompson

CAKES & SOUFFLÉS

There may be no other dessert that symbolizes celebration quite like the cake. It is de rigeur at holidays, birthdays, weddings, funerals, and baptisms—the indispensable centerpiece that encourages sociability, whether the occasion is joyous or tragic. The cake, itself, is a basic concoction and its primary ingredients have always remained the same (with varying proportions as times have waxed prosperous or waned in the other direction). So, if you were looking into a Texan's larder in pioneer times, you'd find on hand the ingredients for a cake—big bags of flour (big enough to piece a dress, if you were enterprising) and 50-pound bags of sugar, too.

Then and now, a cake sets the standard for a polite party—and in Dallas, social gatherings are a vital element in the local scene. So it's not surprising that cakes still command a major influence in the dessert section of Dallas' menus. Elaborating on the possibilities seems to be the guiding sentiment for today's Texas chefs, and you'll find cakes fortified with veins of fudgey intensity; emboldened with tart blackberry puree; and teased with the mysterious nuance of green tea. Flamboyant or demure, the cake remains the darling of dessert chefs.

Green plays a big role at this haute spot for Asian fusion dining—from the splash of color on the wall in the otherwise coolly done up brown and white décor, to the favorite herb referred to in the restaurant's name, to the green tea-infused cake adored by patrons. Despite the strip shopping center location, inside everything seems hip: white oh-so-modern chairs at the counter provide a good view of food and drink prep; gleaming white tables are glamorous; and vegetables are prettily presented and exceptionally fresh.

Owner Nikky Phinyawatana prides herself on imaginative renditions of Chinese, Japanese and Thai classics: soft shell crab has a definite vibe courtesy of a spicy mayonnaise-based dressing; steamed sea bass in lime-ginger sauce scintillates; and any of the offerings that involve Thai red curry are luxurious examples of Phin's reinterpretation of the basics.

And there's a little madness to Phinyawatana's method—Asian Mint is also a coffee and dessert bar. High-end Illy is the coffee of choice. Desserts— pa tong ko, or Asian beignets with sweetened condensed milk as a dipping sauce—are one example of the Phin's vision for pairing Asian flavors with traditional Western pastry-making techniques. It's proved to be a winning combination.

GREEN TEA ICE CREAM CAKE

SERVES 12

ICE CREAM FILLING
2 pints green tea ice cream, slightly softened

GREEN TEA CAKE
2 3/4 cups sifted cake flour
4 teaspoons baking powder
3/4 teaspoon salt
4 large egg whites
1 1/2 cups sugar

3/4 cup unsalted butter, at room temperature
1 cup milk
2 tablespoons Matcha Green Tea Powder, pinch more to dust top

VANILLA FROSTING
8 large egg whites
2 cups sugar
1/2 teaspoon cream of tartar
2 teaspoons vanilla extract

Cover a 9-inch cake pan in plastic wrap with the edges hanging over the outside of the pan. Fill with the green tea ice cream. Smooth and level the top. The ice cream should be about 1/2 inch deep. Cover with another piece of plastic wrap and freeze overnight, or for at least 6 hours.

Preheat the oven to 350° F. Line two 9-inch cake pans with parchment paper.

To make the cake, combine the flour, baking powder, green tea powder, and salt; sift together three times.

In a mixing bowl, beat the egg whites until foamy. Gradually add 1/2 cup of the sugar and continue beating only until soft peaks form.

In another bowl, cream the butter until light and fluffy. Gradually add the remaining 1 cup sugar and beat together until light and fluffy. Add the sifted flour mixture alternately with the milk, a small amount at a time, beating after each addition until smooth. Add the beaten egg whites and fold them into the batter. Spread the batter in the prepared pans.

Bake for 30 to 35 minutes, until a skewer inserted into a cake comes out clean. Cool the cakes in the pans for 10 minutes, then remove from pans and transfer to a wire rack to finish cooling.

To make the frosting, combine the egg whites, sugar, and cream of tartar in the heatproof bowl of an electric mixer. Set over a pan of simmering water. Whisk constantly until the sugar is dissolved and the whites are warm to the touch, 3 to 4 minutes. Transfer the bowl to an electric mixer fitted with the whisk attachment, and beat, starting on low speed, gradually increasing to high, until stiff, glossy peaks form, 5 to 7 minutes. Add the vanilla and mix until combined.

To assemble the cake, level both layers of the cake. Place one layer on a cake board. Remove the green tea ice cream round from the cake pan by removing the top layer of the plastic wrap and pulling evenly on all sides of the bottom plastic wrap to get it out of the pan. If it is too hard, you may use a knife to go around the edge, but be careful not to tear the plastic wrap because it can end up in the cake. Put the ice cream layer on top of the leveled first layer and top with the second leveled layer cake. Frost the top and sides of the cake to your personal design. If you like, you can decorate with extra dusting of green tea matcha powder.

LA DUNI
Cuatro Leches Cake

SERVES 12

DULCE DE LECHE
1 (14-ounce) can Eagle brand condensed milk

VANILLA MANTECADA CAKE
3 cups all-purpose flour
1 1/2 teaspoons baking powder
1/4 teaspoon salt
1 cup unsalted butter, at room temperature
2 cups sugar
4 large eggs
1 teaspoon vanilla extract
1 cup milk

CARAMELIZED MERINGUE
1/2 cup water
2 cups sugar

1 cup egg whites
1 tablespoon fresh lemon juice
1/2 teaspoon vanilla extract

3 LECHES SAUCE
2 cups evaporated milk
2 cups sweetened condensed milk
2 cups whipping cream

AREQUIPE SAUCE
1 cup dulce de leche
1/2 cup whole milk, warmed

Confectioners' sugar, to dust

To make the dulce de leche, put the unopened can inside a large cylinder strainer and submerge the strainer in a large pot of water. Bring the water to a boil over medium-high heat and boil for 2 hours, carefully flipping the can upside down every 45 minutes. Make sure the can is always at least two-thirds covered with water, or it may explode. Remove the can from water, allow to cool to room temperature, then open.

Preheat the oven to 350°F. Butter an 8-inch cake pan and line with parchment paper.

To prepare the cake, sift together the flour, baking powder, and salt.

Cream the butter in an electric mixer fitted with the paddle attachment until very fluffy. Add the sugar gradually, beating until is all incorporated. Add the eggs, one at a time, beating until blended on the lowest speed of the mixer. Continue to mix as you add the vanilla extract, then one-third of the flour mixture. Add half of the milk, then half of the remaining flour mixture, then the rest of milk, then the remaining flour mixture, mixing until the flour is fully incorporated for about 1 minute or less; do not overmix. Pour the batter into the prepared cake pan.

Place the cake in the lower third rack of the oven and bake for 55 to 70 minutes, until the center of the cake springs back when touched and the sides come away from pan. Cool on a wire rack.

To prepare the caramelized meringue, combine the water and sugar in a small saucepan and bring to a boil. Continue to boil until the mixture reaches 240°F (soft-ball stage) on a candy thermometer.

Beat the egg whites in the bowl of an electric mixer fitted with a whip attachment until soft peaks form. Add the sugar syrup slowly as you continue to beat at medium speed. Once the sugar syrup is all incorporated, bring the speed up to high and add lemon juice and vanilla. Continue beating until hard peaks form.

To prepare the 3 Leches Sauce, combine the evaporated milk, condensed milk, and whipping

Who could argue with the La Duni motto: "Where there is cake, there is love."? In fact, who would even want to argue with such a point of view? Certainly not anyone who has sampled the Hazelnut Josefina, a multi-layered fantasy of hazelnut sugar, caramelized phyllo dough pastry, vanilla Bavarian cream, fresh raspberries (when in season), and loads of raspberry coulis.

However, cake is not the only attraction here. In fact, this bakery also is a restaurant, a catering company, and a bar. It's known all over town for its creative blend of European tradition with Latin American soul—and it hosts tea parties, too. La Duni's three-tier service includes a variety of sweets, tea pastries, finger sandwiches, and exotic teas. Party favors, crystallized fruits and flowers, plus sugar place cards are, well, icing on the cake.

Owner and executive pastry chef Dunia Borga works with her husband, Taco Borga, in this always-lively setting, to create interesting sandwiches, salads (a grilled asparagus version is a scene-stealer), and sides (yucca fries are irresistible). And, if that's not enough, D Magazine has declared La Duni's "the best cocktails in Dallas."

cream. Whisk together until well blended. Refrigerate.

To prepare the Arequipe Sauce, whisk together 1 cup of the dulce de leche with the milk until well blended. Refrigerate.

To assemble the dessert, turn the cake out onto an 8-inch round of cardboard and remove the parchment paper. Slice the cake horizontally into three even layers, using toothpicks to guide your knife. Pierce each layer with a fork to allow the sauce to sink into the cake. Brush 3/4 cup of the 3 Leches Sauce onto each layer, making sure each layer is moist as you top the layers and reassemble the cake. Using a spatula, spread the meringue over the sides and top of the cake, making sure to create a 1/2-inch-thick cover all around the cake. Finish with decorative peaks. Torch the meringue until golden brown, making sure not to burn it. Drizzle the cake with the Arequipe Sauce and dust with confectioners' sugar.

THE LANDMARK
CHOCOLATE STOUT CAKE WITH STOUT GANACHE

SERVES 6

Located on the first floor of the historic Warwick Melrose Hotel, this delightful space is flooded with sunlight that streams through the arched windows in the daytime. At night, its European-style elegance establishes a mood that's formal without being faux. It might be the crisp white linens on the tables, or the flattering light that emanates from the wall sconces, or the comfortably grand upholstered dining chairs—but diners look good and feel good here.

It doesn't hurt that the menu offerings are as delightful as the setting—knowing combinations (lemon-infused crab cakes with grapefruit-brown butter and smoked tomato puree) inspire diners. Piquant pairings, such as the charred tomato bisque with balsamic vinegar, are a bracing option at Sunday brunch. And the breakfasts here are famous for getting the routine business meeting off to an impressive start—try the grilled tenderloin filet with farm fresh eggs over a crispy potato cake with demi glace.

CAKE
2 cups all-purpose flour
1 cup granulated sugar
1 cup firmly packed light brown sugar
1 1/2 teaspoons baking powder
1 teaspoon salt
1 cup Rouge Stout beer, or any good stout beer
3/4 cup dark or Dutch-processed unsweetened cocoa powder
1 cup unsalted butter
2 large eggs
1/2 cup sour cream

STOUT GANACHE
12 ounces semisweet chocolate chips
1/3 cup unsalted butter
1/2 cup Rouge Stout beer
1/4 cup corn syrup
1/2 cup heavy cream

Ice cream, to serve

Preheat the oven to 325° F. Spray a 10-inch round or 12-inch by 8-inch rectangle baking dish with nonstick spray and line with waxed paper.

To prepare the cake, sift together the flour, granulated sugar, brown sugar, baking powder, and salt into a large mixing bowl and set aside.

Combine the stout, cocoa, and butter in a heatproof bowl. Set the bowl over a pot of boiling water and heat until the butter is fully melted.

Add the eggs, sour cream, and the stout mixture to the flour mixture and mix until just combined well; do not overwork the batter. Spoon into the prepared cake pan.

Bake the cake for 20 to 25 minutes, until a toothpick inserted in the center comes out clean. Cool on a wire rack.

To make the ganache, combine the chocolate chips, butter, stout, and corn syrup in the top of a double boiler over barely simmering water. Cook, stirring, until the chocolate is melted and smooth. Meanwhile heat the cream until hot and add to the chocolate mixture. Mix well to combine. Hold in a warm spot.

While the cake is still warm, cut into six equal portions. Serve each piece with the sauce and a scoop of ice cream.

PIES & TARTS

Leave it to Americans to take a nice, staid English tradition and run wild with it. The pie is a staple of cooking, raised to an art form in England as the basis for one of the original take-away foods. Meat pies, steak and cheese, steak and kidney, minced meats and mushroom are hearty versions and, of course, the pot pie is the ultimate comfort food.

But in the United States an abundance of fruits such as blueberries, blackberries, apples, peaches, cherries, lemons, and raspberries present irresistible opportunity to enlarge upon a classic. The availability of more exotic fruit options, such as key limes and coconut, is permission to dream big—and so we do, with coconut, lemon, and chocolate pies crowned with mountainous meringue. Enthusiastic cooks do not shy away from excess, either, further adorning these creations with sprinkles of toasted coconut, slices of lemon, or chocolate chips.

The pie—and its mini-version, the tart—has always seemed like a happy dessert. It's a celebration of nature's abundance, comes out of the oven bubbling and fragrant, and is the only dessert you can get away with eating morning, noon, or night.

AL BIERNAT'S
Texas Pecan Pie à la Mode

SERVES 8

PECAN PIE
2 cups light corn syrup
10 tablespoons cake flour
1 tablespoon sugar
1 cup eggs
4 tablespoons plus 1 teaspoon unsalted butter, softened
1 tablespoon vanilla extract
1 cup pecan pieces
1 (10-inch) unbaked pie shell

VANILLA SAUCE
2 cups milk
1/2 vanilla bean
1/2 cup plus 1 tablespoon sugar
5 large egg yolks

CHOCOLATE SAUCE
1 1/4 cups water
3/4 cup plus 2 tablespoons sugar
3 1/2 tablespoons unsalted butter
1 cup unsweetened cocoa powder
11 ounces semisweet chocolate, chopped into small pieces

CARAMEL SAUCE
1 2/3 cups sugar
6 tablespoons water
2 cups heavy cream
1 tablespoon vanilla extract

Vanilla bean ice cream, to serve.

Preheat the oven to 350°F.

To prepare the pie, combine the corn syrup, cake flour, sugar, eggs, butter, and vanilla in a mixing bowl and stir in the pecans. Pour the mixture into the pie shell. Bake for 35 to 45 minutes, until the edges are firm and the center is still quivery. Let cool on a wire rack for about 1 1/2 hours.

To prepare the chocolate sauce, combine the water, sugar and butter in a small saucepan and bring to a boil over medium-high heat. Whisk in the cocoa powder until fully dissolved. Remove from the heat and stir in the chocolate, a little at a time, until all is incorporated. The sauce may be served hot or cold. (Makes 4 cups.)

To prepare the caramel sauce, combine the sugar and water in a heavy saucepan over medium-high heat and stir with a wooden spoon until the sugar dissolves and the mixture comes to a boil. Clean the sugar splatters on the sides of the pan with a pastry brush and water to prevent crystallization. Continue cooking until the sugar caramelizes and the mixture is dark brown. Remove from heat and immediately add the cream in a slow steady stream. Whisk until completely blended. Stir in the vanilla. Cool in refrigerator. Serve either warm or cold. (Makes 3 cups.)

To prepare the vanilla sauce, combine the sugar and egg yolks in a bowl and whisk until pale and fluffy. Bring the milk and vanilla bean to a boil in a saucepan over medium-high heat. Slowly add to the egg yolk mixture, whisking constantly. Return the mixture to saucepan and cook, stirring continuously, until mixture thickens enough to coat the back of a spoon. Cool the custard quickly by pouring it into an ice bath. Remove the vanilla bean. When cool, strain through a fine-mesh strainer. Scrape the seeds from the vanilla bean into the sauce and stir occasionally until completely cooled. Serve cold. (Makes 5 cups).

Serve the pie at room temperature with the ice cream and finish with swirls of chocolate sauce, caramel sauce, and vanilla sauce.

In a city that could reasonably be called steak-crazy, this restaurant distinguishes itself. That's partly because owner Al Biernat's philosophy of food preparation comes from his 30 years in the food service industry. He offers the basics, dolls them up with spectacular salads and interesting side dishes, and then bowls over his customers with sensational desserts. As if that's not enough, the wine list here is a winning combination of all the big California names with a few real stunners thrown in—all at a good price.

But perhaps the biggest draw at this steakhouse is Al Biernat himself. Host to a well-dressed crowd that often consists of players from the Mavericks, the Stars, and the Cowboys sports teams; visiting celebrities like Julio Iglesias; and local big shots such as Southwest Airlines owner Herb Kelleher, Biernat is without equal when it comes to hospitality. Because of that, power brokers love this place and many a deal has been sealed here over a hunky ribeye or 25-ounce cowboy steak. Success is even sweeter thanks to pastry chef Guadalupe Vega's skilled touch that has made this chophouse just as famous for its desserts as it is for the meat.

Dean Fearing is revered for more than his ground-breaking contribution to Southwestern cooking. His expansive personality, generosity, and penchant for Lucchese boots are traits that have expunged snobbishness from the world of fine dining according to Fearing. His namesake restaurant is located in the brand new Robert A.M. Stern Ritz-Carlton in the newly developed Uptown section of Dallas, and foodies from all over the world clamor for reservations to dine in one of the rawhide chandelier-lit dining rooms, at the chef's table, on the terrace, or under the vaulted stone ceiling in the wine cellar. Die-hard fans insist that the kitchen's ringside seating can't be beat.

After 20-plus years at The Mansion on Turtle Creek, Fearing is now developing a new generation of highly flavorful dishes, and it's paying off. Esquire magazine named Fearing's America's Restaurant of the Year in 2007. Scallops with tangerine essence and the chicken-fried Maine lobster with queso fresco mashed potatoes are favorite new offerings; but still on the menu is the tortilla soup, Fearing's most famous creation. No detail is left to chance here, and the result makes a big statement—and that's what Fearing has based his reputation on.

FEARING'S
CARAMELIZED APPLE FRITTERS

SERVES 6

CARAMELIZED APPLES
1/2 cup granulated sugar
2 apples, peeled and finely diced
1/2 teaspoon ground cinnamon

FRITTER BATTER
1 1/2 cups all-purpose flour
1/4 cup granulated sugar
1 teaspoon ground cinnamon
1 whole vanilla bean, split and scraped
1/2 teaspoon finely grated lemon zest
2 large eggs, separated
1/2 cup whole milk
2 teaspoons unsalted butter, melted

Oil for deep-frying
Cinnamon sugar
Caramel sauce (any quality commercial variety),
  warmed

To prepare the caramelized apples, heat the sugar in a medium saucepan over medium-high heat until melted. Carefully add the apples and cinnamon; cook until the apples are tender and the cooking liquid is dark brown, about 5 minutes. Set aside to cool. Then drain and set aside for the fritter batter.

To prepare the fritter batter, combine the flour, sugar, cinnamon, seeds from the vanilla bean, and lemon zest in a bowl. Set aside.

Combine the egg yolks, milk, and melted butter in a small bowl. Slowly add to the flour mixture, whisking constantly to avoid lumps.

Beat the egg whites in a clean bowl until they are stiff and glossy. Fold into the batter.

Heat the oil in a deep-fryer or tall saucepan to 350°F. Preheat the oven to 250°F

Fold the strained apples into the fritter batter. Using a 3/4-ounce ice-cream scoop or a large spoon, add a few scoops to the oil and fry until dark brown and puffed. Remove from the oil, drain briefly on paper towels, then roll in cinnamon sugar. Repeat until all the batter is used. Keep the fritters in the warm oven while you continue to fry in batches.

To serve, place three fritters on each plate and top with your favorite caramel sauce.

KITCHEN 1924
COCONUT CREAM PIE

SERVES 6 TO 8

2 1/2 cups milk
2/3 cup sugar
1/2 teaspoon salt
6 large egg yolks
1/2 cup cornstarch
5 tablespoons unsalted butter, at room
  temperature

1 1/4 cups toasted coconut flakes, plus more
  for topping
1/2 vanilla bean
Baked 9-inch pie shell
1 ounce white chocolate
Whipped cream, to serve

Combine the milk, 1/3 cup of the sugar, and salt into a heavy-bottomed saucepan. Split the vanilla bean and scrape the seeds into the pan; discard the bean. Place over medium-high heat and whisk for a minute or so to combine. Heat the mixture until it just begins to boil, stirring occasionally.

Meanwhile, whisk together the eggs and the remaining 1/3 cup sugar in a medium mixing bowl until well combined. Then, in two equal parts, add the cornstarch and beat until the eggs are smooth, thick, and pale.

Pour a very small amount of the hot milk mixture into the eggs, whisking constantly. Very slowly add the remaining milk to the eggs, whisking steadily until thoroughly combined and return to the saucepan. If for some reason it clumps a little, you can easily sieve the mixture and return to the saucepan.

Cook over medium-low heat, whisking constantly to ensure a smooth, homogeneous custard. When the mix begins to thicken, decrease the heat to low and keep stirring vigorously until it reaches a pudding consistency.

Remove the pan from the heat and pour the custard into a mixing bowl set in an ice bath to stop the cooking process. After it's cooled down a little, stir in the butter until mixed well. Stir in the coconut flakes.

Press a sheet of plastic wrap against the surface of the custard to prevent a skin from forming, and refrigerate for 3 to 4 hours, until well chilled.

Melt the white chocolate in the top of a double boiler over barely simmering water. Brush a thin layer of white chocolate inside the pie shell. Spoon the custard into pie shell. Top with whipped cream and toasted coconut flakes.

The food at this long, narrow eatery is all about comfort—but comfort as defined by someone who's a little wacky and has a hearty sense of humor. There's just enough space for the wait staff to wend their way past tables lined up along both walls, but patrons don't seem to mind the no-frills, close quarters—they pack the place to see what surprises are in store from the kitchen.

Deviled eggs are a trademark dish here, sometimes filled with smoked salmon or tasso ham; other times, these devilish delights are made in the original style, the kind you'd pack up and take on a Sunday outing. Specialties of the house center around roasted meats and fish—don't miss the seared scallops—and are always accompanied by well-thought-out side dishes such as warm blue cheese potato salad or sweet potato au gratin.

Devotees look forward to the holiday season because Kitchen 1924 then offers a catering menu: trays of side dishes are popular for parties or for family and friends when you feel like celebrating with comfort food with a gourmet opinion.

HECTOR'S ON HENDERSON
WHITE CHOCOLATE BANANA
MOON PIE

SERVES 8

1 package (3 ½-ounce size) vanilla pudding
(not instant)
1 cup white chocolate chips
1/4 cup granulated sugar
4 cups heavy whipping cream
4 bananas
8 Moon Pies
1 cup strawberries, hulled
1 cup blueberries
1/4 cup honey
Chocolate sauce

Follow the package directions for making pudding with the pudding mix and milk. While the pudding is still warm, fold in the white chocolate until completely blended. Chill.

Combine the sugar and heavy cream in a large bowl and whip until soft peaks form. Fold half of the whipped cream into the pudding. Return to the refrigerator.

Just before serving, peel and cut the bananas into 1/4-inch slices. Split the Moon Pies in half horizontally. Place banana slices on the bottom half of all the Moon pies. Spoon the pudding mixture evenly on top of the banana slices. Place the tops on the Moon Pies. Pipe the remaining whipped cream on top of the closed Moon Pies. Garnish with the berries and pour honey and your favorite chocolate sauce over all.

Housed in the old Potter Iron Works in the happening Knox-Henderson section of town, Hector's operates on the theory that eating good food should be an experience that's accompanied by good music. The notion comes alive—literally—every night when jazz performers take the stage around 7. It's a concept that's been a hit: Gourmet *magazine selected Hector's as one of just six Dallas restaurants they recommend in the November 2005 issue. In 2008,* D Magazine *named it one of the best neighborhood restaurants in the city.*

The stylish, vibrant restaurant is the brainchild of Cuban-born Hector Garcia. Guests have come to know their host because he's always on hand to greet diners when they arrive. Hector is also an actor, and locals may remember his exuberant performance as the number 9 on televised lottery drawings. His enthusiasm shows in the carefully selected offerings on the menu, too.

Texas Monthly *magazine pronounced the grilled snapper atop a white-bean puree with tomatoes Provencal on the side an "absolute taste sensation." Executive chef Blythe Beck makes sure other dishes measure up: chicken-fried chicken livers with caramelized cipolline onions on mixed greens is topped with a Blackstrap molasses vinaigrette and is definitely good for what ails you.*

Proudly stuck firmly in the 1950's, this local favorite has prospered in one of the city's great old-fashioned outdoor shopping malls. Owners Marc and Susan Hall bought the place in 1989, but the barbecue tradition was long established at this location which housed Howard and Peggy's for over 40 years and the Peggy's Beef Bar before it closed in 1989. The original menu from Howard and Peggy's is still in the window for those who want to compare then and now.

Actually, "now" may be healthier: Peggy Sue BBQ is known for other things besides meat. The sides are a big attraction. A piquant vinegar-based slaw is a saucy antidote to the slow-cooked, brown-sugar crusted ribs and lean brisket; spinach or squash casseroles are hearty accompaniments too. But purists out there may prefer pairing the three meat platter with mashed potatoes, flavorful fries, or buttermilk-battered, medium-thick onion rings. Just don't forget that the place is famous for homemade pies and fried pies—and it's incumbent upon the discerning diner to find out why.

PEGGY SUE BBQ
FRIED APRICOT PIE

SERVES 8

2 cups self-rising flour
1/3 cup vegetable shortening
2/3 cup ice-cold water
6 ounces dried apricots
1 cup sugar
1/4 teaspoon ground allspice or ground
   cinnamon
Oil for deep-frying
Confectioners' sugar

Combine the flour and shortening in the bowl of a food processor. Pulse several times until the mixture resembles cornmeal. Sprinkle with ice water and pulse briefly, until the water is mixed into the dough. Remove the dough from the bowl, form into a ball, cover with plastic wrap and allow to rest for 30 minutes.

Dice the apricots into 1/2-inch pieces. Put in a heavy saucepan and cover with water. Cover and simmer until almost all the liquid has evaporated. Add the sugar and spice and stir over low heat until dissolved. Remove from the heat and let cool.

To assemble, divide the pastry into eight portions. On a floured board, roll each into a 6- inch circle. Place 1/4 cup of filling in the center, moisten the edges with a little water, and fold the pastry circles in half. Press the edges with a fork dipped in flour. Cook immediately or freeze. Frozen pies are much easier to work with because they are less fragile.

Heat the oil in a deep-fryer or tall saucepan to 375°F. Fry fresh pies for about 3 minutes, or until golden brown. Frozen pies should be fried without defrosting, for about 4 minutes. To cook in a large skillet, use about 1/2 inch of corn oil, and fry the pies over medium-high heat for about 3 minutes on each side.

Drain the cooked pies on paper towels, dust with confectioners' sugar, and serve while nice and warm.

Note: You can substitute any dried fruit, or you can use canned pie filling, as long as it is not runny.

STRAWBERRY TART WITH GRAND MARNIER BAVARIAN

SERVES 8

TART SHELL
3 1/3 cups cake flour
3/4 cup plus 1 1/2 tablespoons sugar
1 1/8 cups unsalted butter, chilled and cubed
2 large eggs
1/2 teaspoon vanilla extract

GRAND MARNIER CREAM FILLING
4 cups whole milk
1 1/4 cups plus 2 1/2 tablespoons sugar
1 cup eggs (5 large)

3 1/2 tablespoons arrowroot powder
6 tablespoons unsalted butter
2 cups whipping cream
2 tablespoons Grand Marnier liqueur

GARNISH
2 pints fresh strawberries, halved
1/4 cup toasted sliced almonds
Shaved chocolate
Edible glitter (optional)

Can there ever be too much of a good thing? Not at this charming Parisian-style bakery in the heart of Dallas' Deep Ellum. Sky blue walls, chocolate brown accents, French lighting, little replicas of the Eiffel Tower on every table, and art on display make an inviting environment for busy city dwellers to stop whatever they are doing and enjoy life. The two-room café opens early—sleepyheads can be revived with owner Samantha Rush's rich Italian coffee and her renowned light and flaky croissants. Another breakfast option is a handmade (like every confection sold here) blueberry, cranberry-orange, or lemon poppy seed muffin—packed with fresh fruit and sprinkled with hunky sugar crystals.

Of course, most offerings are oh-so-French: pates de fruit, palmiers, lunettes, sable Breton shortbreads, Madeleines, chausson aux pommes, and that old standby—quiche. Macaroons and financiers are the latest additions. Dieters appreciate that most break-fast and pastries are also available in petite versions, which confirms that quality, not quantity, is what's important here.

To prepare the tart shell, combine the flour, sugar, and butter in the bowl of an electric mixer with the paddle attachment. Beat until the mixture looks sandy, like cornmeal. Add the eggs and vanilla, and continue mixing until a dough is formed. Wrap the dough in plastic wrap and chill for 30 minutes.

Preheat the oven to 350°F.

Roll out the dough on a lightly floured surface to thickness of 1/4 inch. Line two 8-inch or eight 4-inch tart pans with removable bottoms with the dough. Fill the tart shells with pie weights.

Bake the tart shells for 18 to 22 minutes, until golden brown. Cool on wire racks.

To make the filling, combine the milk and 3/4 cups of the sugar in a small saucepan and bring to a boil.

Meanwhile, whisk together the eggs, arrowroot, and 1/2 cup sugar. Very slowly pour in the milk mixture, whisking constantly. Return the mixture to the saucepan and cook over low heat, stirring continuously, until the mixture thickens. Transfer to a bowl and whisk in the butter until completely melted. Place plastic wrap on the surface of the cream and refrigerate the mixture until cold.

While the mixture is cooling, whip the whipping cream with the remaining 2 1/2 tablespoons sugar until firm peaks form. Refrigerate the whipped cream until you are ready to assemble the tart.

To assemble the tart, remove the tart shell from the tart pan. Whisk the Grand Marnier into the chilled pastry cream. Then, lightly fold the sweetened whipped cream into the mixture, reserving a small amount of the whipped cream for garnish. Fill the tart shell with the Grand Marnier Cream. Arrange the strawberry halves on top. Garnish the tart with whipped cream, toasted almonds, shaved chocolate, and edible glitter.

SALUM
CHOCOLATE TART

SERVES 12

CRUST
1/2 cup toasted almonds
1/2 cup graham cracker crumbs
1/4 cup sugar
3 tablespoons melted unsalted butter

FILLING
1 1/2 cups unsalted butter
3/4 cup water
3/4 cup sugar
Pinch of salt
16 ounces semisweet chocolate chips
6 large egg yolks

RASPBERRY COULIS
8 ounces frozen raspberries
1/4 cup sugar
1 1/2 teaspoons lemon juice

GARNISH
Caramel sauce
Fresh berries
Fresh mint

Preheat the oven to 350° F. Line a 9-inch springform pan with parchment paper.

To prepare the crust, mix together the almonds, graham cracker crumbs, sugar, and butter. Put into the prepared pan and pat to form an even layer along the bottom and up the sides of the pan. Bake for about 10 minutes, until lightly toasted. Cool on a wire rack.

Preheat a convection or conventional oven to 325° F.

To prepare the filling, combine the butter, water, sugar, and salt in a saucepan and bring to a full boil. Pour over the chocolate chips in a bowl and whisk until fully blended. Stir in the egg yolks. Pour into the crust.

Bake (in the convection oven with blower on low) for 5 to 7 minutes, or until the filling starts to bubble around the edges. Cool overnight in the refrigerator.

To prepare the coulis, combine the raspberries, sugar, and lemon juice in a small saucepan over medium heat. Bring to a boil, then reduce the heat and simmer until the sugar dissolves, the raspberries burst, and the liquid reduces by half, about 15 minutes. Strain the raspberries through a fine-mesh strainer and discard solids. Reserve the coulis in a nonreactive container until you are ready to serve. (The coulis will keep for 2 weeks, if refrigerated.)

To slice, cut the tart into twelve pieces. Serve with a drizzle of caramel sauce and raspberry coulis. Garnish with fresh berries and mint.

Located in that glamorous niche between haute Highland Park and trendy Uptown, Salum is the epitome of its owner/chef Abraham Salum's sensibilities. The spacious dining room seats 85, and nearly every one of the seats provides a good view of Salum and his staff at work in the sleek, open kitchen. Tones of brown, green and beige cast an understated background for the sexy minimalism that progressive Dallas interior designer Julio Quinones is known for—but it also is a backdrop for the city's foodies, who seem to have flocked to this place instinctively. Not disappointed by what they found, these well-informed, fashionable trendsetters (who could be fickle if they wanted to) have stuck around.

Chef Salum specializes in contemporary American cuisine that varies month to month as well as by season. Fans will remember him from his four years at nearby Parigi but now that he presides over his own kitchen, this graduate of the New England Culinary Institute has come into his own. His experience in kitchens in France, Belgium, and Mexico contributes to an imaginative menu. Salum is unfalteringly cordial to guests, and pairs the jobs of greeter and chef with élan.

THREE CITRUS PIE

SERVES 8

PIE SHELL
1 1/2 cups finely crushed graham cracker crumbs
1/2 cup sugar
1/4 cup unsalted butter, melted

FILLING
6 large egg yolks
6 tablespoons fresh orange juice
6 tablespoons fresh lemon juice
6 tablespoons fresh lime juice
2 (14-ounce) cans Eagle brand sweetened condensed milk

Whipped cream, to garnish
Thinly sliced citrus fruit, to garnish

Preheat the oven to 450°F.

To prepare the crust, combine the graham cracker crumbs, sugar, and butter in a medium bowl and mix well. Press evenly along the bottom and up the sides of a 10-inch pie plate. Bake for 10 minutes. Let cool.

Decrease the oven temperature to 350°F.

To prepare the filling, beat the egg yolks in an electric mixer on low speed until just blended. With the motor running, slowly pour in each juice in a thin stream. Let set for 5 minutes, then gradually stir in condensed milk. Pour into the cooled crust.

Bake for 20 minutes. Let cool completely on a wire rack, then chill. Garnish each slice with whipped cream and a thin slice of citrus fruit. The dessert shown also is garnished with a raspberry sauce—use your favorite commercial one, or see page 46 for raspberry coulis recipe.

Located on the thoroughfare leading right into the heart of the posh Park Cities, Sevy's is that rare combination—a restaurant that is the perfect place to seal a deal, but also a neighborhood restaurant frequented by families with children, grandparents, and friends in tow. It's been so popular for so long that D Magazine placed it on its "Best of Dallas" honor roll. Regular patrons even have little brass plaques marking their favorite tables.

Chef-owner Jim Severson, for whom Sevy's is named, maintains a high profile here and is often seen in his chef's white and golf shoes (minus the spikes) chatting with diners. That doesn't mean he's neglecting the food, though: fresh and homemade is the hallmark. Corn chowder redolent of sweet corn, celery, cream and spices is a signature dish. Classics usually come with a twist, such as their rendition of roast chicken—here, it's grilled with rosemary; barbecued salmon tweaked with Tabasco butter and sided with crispy leeks and a mound of buttermilk-chive mashed potatoes is a crowd-pleaser. Severson is best known, though, for herb-marinated grilled lamb chops, which are at their best when medium-rare.

For guests used to making those big deals at the golf course, Severson indulges them with a compact putting green located on the patio.

T ROOM AT FORTY-FIVE TEN
LEMON PISTACHIO TART

SERVES 12

TART PASTRY DOUGH
2 1/2 cups all-purpose flour
1/2 cup confectioners' sugar
1 cup unsalted butter, chilled and diced

PISTACHIO FILLING
1/2 cup unsalted butter, chilled and diced
1/2 cup granulated sugar
1 cup pistachios
1 large egg

LEMON TOPPING
6 large egg yolks
1 cup granulated sugar
1/2 cup fresh lemon juice
1 teaspoon finely grated lemon zest
1/2 cup unsalted butter

Preheat the oven to 325°F.

To prepare the tart shell, mix together the flour and confectioners' sugar until well blended. Cut in the butter until the mixture resembles coarse meal. Form into a ball. On a lightly floured surface, roll out to fit a 10-inch tart pan. Transfer to the pan and trim the edges. Fill with pie weights or dried beans and bake for 15 minutes, until golden.

While the tart crust pastry bakes, prepare the filling. Combine the butter, sugar, pistachios, and egg in a food processor and pulse for about 30 seconds. Evenly spread the pistachio mixture onto the tart shell.

Bake for 20 minutes. Cool on a wire rack.

To prepare the lemon topping, combine the egg yolks, granulated sugar, lemon juice, lemon zest, and butter in the top of a double boiler over boiling water. Whisk until the mixture thickens and coats the back of a spoon. Chill for 1 hour, until set. Then pour over the tart. Return to the refrigerator and chill overnight. Then enjoy!

A little bird (a yellow one, the signature of this swanky venue) tells us that mixing shopping and dining can be a satisfying combination, especially when it's a fashionable enterprise that was named by Lucky *magazine "one of the top 10 boutiques in the country" for 2007. This restaurant has attracted the attention of the likes of Gwyneth Paltrow, Oprah Winfrey and Erykah Badu, and has been featured in publications galore.* Town & Country, Elle Décor, In Style, *and* The New York Times *just can't say enough about what's cooking in this 8,000-square-foot store—both fashion-wise and in the T Room café.*

The renovated historic building opens onto a court-yard and fountain, making the airy and fresh environment ideal for browsing stationery by Mrs. John L. Strong; teas and candles from Le Palais des Thes; luxurious organic linens by Anna Sova; gold bangles by Ippolita; Y3 shoes; Alexander McQueen handbags; and clothing by Derek Lam, Dries Van Noten and Givenchy.

So much style, though, is bound to whet one's appetite—and owners Shelly Musselman and Brian Bolke understand that good taste comes in many shapes, sizes and flavors. Soups, salads, and an ever-changing array of entrees beckon; the panini is always in demand, and the brisk cappuccino braces shoppers who know they must forge on.

CENTRAL 214
INSIDE-OUT KEY LIME PIE

SERVES 8

GRAHAM CRACKER CRUST
2/3 cup graham cracker crumbs
1 1/2 tablespoons sugar
Pinch of kosher salt
3 tablespoons unsalted butter, melted

KEY LIME FILLING
7 ounces (3/4 cup plus 2 tablespoons) sweetened condensed milk
2 large egg yolks
1/4 cup Key lime juice
Zest of 1 lime

RASPBERRY COULIS
1 pint fresh raspberries
1/2 cup sugar
3 tablespoons water

Fresh berries to garnish
Whipped cream, to garnish

Situated at the corner of Mockingbird and the major thoroughfare that goes past SMU and NorthPark Shopping Center, and connects the pricey Park Cities to upscale Lakewood, Central 214 couldn't be more at the center of things. Or of 214, the Dallas area code. It's in the recently renovated boutique Hotel Palomar—both the restaurant and hotel have been stylishly decorated in burnt sienna, jade, olive and emerald greens by Paul Draper, Dallas' master of understated American elegance.

The open kitchen grants the chef final say on every dish en route to the dining room. Conversely, guests get the panorama of the chef and his staff at work—two bar-height tables, each seating 10 people, are positioned in front of the kitchen and offer a fine vantage point. For those who prefer less interaction, the flagstone terrace and its surrounding garden offer a way to enjoy the pleasures of being served.

The nightly menu features slow cooking on the exhibition rotisserie—steak, chicken, pork, seafood, and wild game are the beneficiaries of this carefully thought-out technique.

Preheat the oven to 300°F.

To prepare the crust, combine the crumbs, sugar, and salt in food processor and process to mix. With the motor running, slowly add the melted butter. Form a crust in eight 6-ounce ceramic baking dishes. Bake for about 15 minutes, until golden brown. Let cool. Then chill in refrigerator for 2 hours

Preheat the oven to 300°F.

To prepare the filling, combine the condensed milk, egg yolks, lime juice, and lime zest in a medium bowl and whisk until smooth. Fill the crusts with the key lime filling, cover, and refrigerate overnight. Bake 15 minutes. Refrigerate for 1 to 2 hours.

To make the raspberry coulis, combine the raspberries, sugar, and water in a small saucepan over low heat. Cook just until the sugar dissolves, stirring constantly. Puree the mixture, then strain and let cool.

To assemble the dessert, brush each serving plate with the raspberry coulis using a pastry brush. Invert one of the ceramic dishes onto each plate and gently remove the dish. Garnish with fresh berries and whipped cream.

PUDDINGS & CUSTARDS

Custard, or pudding, probably came to Texas courtesy of French, Spanish, and English settlers—we've made the most of the creamy, milk-and-egg-based concoction ever since. It's the ultimate in adaptability, a handy vehicle for home cooks and virtuoso chefs alike to show off their knowledge and skill.

Not all custards are sweet, of course. There's the quiche, which is simply a savory custard tart, and some versions of the timbale or dreaded meatloaf are custard-based. But Texans as a group, and Dallasites as one of the most flamboyant subsets, have a collective sweet tooth and just love to see the custard done up in as many sugary ways as possible. That's why puddings can range from the demure to the downright wild.

Everything is bigger and better in Texas, or so we like to say. This holds true for puddings and custards; throw in a few more ingredients such as bread and a dash of rum, and you've got a killer bread pudding. It's a treatment that makes the most out of a little, but that's also why a custard base is the starting point for so many of our best desserts.

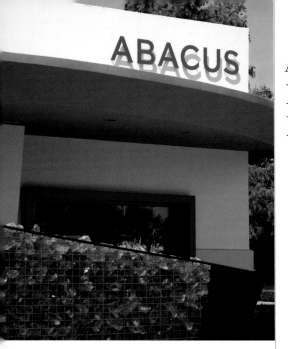

Lemon Brioche–Peach Bread Pudding

SERVES 8

1 small loaf (approximately 8 ounces) brioche
  or challah
2 cups heavy cream
1 cup whole milk
1/2 cup sugar, plus additional sugar to sprinkle
Pinch of salt
Zest of 2 lemons
8 large egg yolks
4 peaches, peeled, pitted, and halved
Whipped cream or ice cream, to serve

Preheat the oven to 350° F. Lightly brush softened butter on the bottom and sides of eight 8-ounce ramekins and set aside.

Slice the bread and cut into circles that fit into the ramekins. The thickness of the bread slices will determine how many you need for each ramekin. Place the slices on a sheet pan and allow to dry out a bit while preparing custard.

To prepare the custard, heat the cream and milk in a saucepan until scalded. Remove from the heat and add the lemon zest and allow to steep for 30 minutes. Strain the zest from the cream mixture, return the cream mixture to the saucepan, and heat until bubbles appear around the edges of the pan. Remove from the heat and add 1/4 cup of the sugar and salt.

In the top of a double boiler, whisk the remaining 1/4 cup sugar into the egg yolks. Very slowly stir the hot cream into the yolks, whisking constantly. Place the top of a double boiler over slowly simmering water and stir with a wooden spoon until slightly thickened and coats the back of a spoon. (This is a classic crème anglaise that is used for ice cream and baked custards.)

To assemble the bread pudding, placing one circle of brioche in the bottom of each ramekin. Pour a small amount of custard on the brioche to moisten, add another slice and more custard. Allow enough room in the top of the ramekins to finish with a peach half, skin side up. Make sure there is plenty of custard in the bread or it will be dry. Sprinkle the top of the peach with sugar.

Place the ramekins in a deep pan and add water to the pan to fill it halfway up the sides of the ramekins. Cover the whole pan with foil and punch a couple of small holes to allow steam to escape. Bake for about 30 minutes. Remove the foil and continue to bake for about 15 minutes, until the custard is set and golden brown on top.

Serve warm with whipped cream or ice cream.

Chef and owner Kent Rathbun is a bigger-than-life character, and even those people who haven't been to his restaurant or tasted his award-winning food know the celebrity and his brother, Kevin, as the team that defeated Bobby Flay on Iron Chef America. Kent has been cooking since he was 17, and has garnered awards galore: Bon Appetit *magazine's Best of the Year 2001 issue named Abacus' chef's tasting menu a top pick, and* USA Today's *food critic Jerry Shriver claims to have found at Abacus one of the top meals in the world.*

"I want everyone that experiences Abacus to feel as if they are a guest in my home," declares Rathbun. And actually, his own home is available for private parties and art events. The chef loves to travel and visit kitchens in other restaurants—the result is an imaginative menu shaped by Mediterranean, Cajun/Creole, Southwestern, and Pacific Rim influences.

Diners in the know will choose the chef's table set at the bow of Rathbun's European-style kitchen. From here Rathbun's fans get the full view of all the chefs at work preparing the nine courses on the tasting menu, with wine pairings.

The high and mighty have strutted through this Beaux Arts building, erected in 1923 when this now-bustling area near downtown was a quiet, tree-lined suburb. Maria Callas, Judy Garland, Elvis Presley, Andy Warhol and Frank Lloyd Wright were guests in the hotel's heyday. And now, after a mega-million dollar renovation, the Stoneleigh and its restaurant are again in the spotlight.

Executive chef David Bull, who learned food preparation alongside his grandparents in their up-state New York Italian restaurant, has reinterpreted those vivid memories into a new version of modern Italian cooking. Garlic-chive gnocchi, oyster gazpacho, and veal cheek piccata finesse tradition and turn it into inspiration. It's no wonder that Bull has been repeatedly lavished with awards and was a James Beard "Best New Chef in the Southwest" nominee for 2007.

But pretty is as pretty does, and in Bolla the setting is part of the fun. Dark wood floors, off-white luxe leather banquettes and leather chairs, and oversized color photographs showcased on the white walls are a dramatic and elegant revival of a space with a genuinely glamorous past.

BOLLA
POMEGRANATE PANNA COTTA WITH RED WINE GELÉE

SERVES 8

POMEGRANATE PANNA COTTA
1 tablespoon plus 1 teaspoon unflavored gelatin
2 cups pomegranate juice
1/2 cup fresh orange juice
1/2 cup heavy cream
1 1/2 cups buttermilk
1 cup sugar
Zest of 1 orange

RED WINE GELÉE
2 1/2 tablespoons unflavored gelatin
3 cups red wine
1/2 cup corn syrup
1/4 cup sugar

POMEGRANATE SAUCE
2 cups pomegranate juice
1 cup sugar
Zest of 1 orange

TUILES
5 tablespoons unsalted butter, at room temperature
1 cup confectioners' sugar
2 large egg whites
1/2 cup all-purpose flour
1/2 teaspoon vanilla extract

Micro mint, to garnish

To prepare the panna cotta, sprinkle the gelatin over 1/4 cup of the pomegranate juice in a small bowl and set aside.

Whisk together the orange juice, cream, and buttermilk in a bowl and set aside.

Combine the sugar, remaining 1 3/4 cups pomegranate juice, and orange zest in a medium saucepan over medium-high heat and bring to a rolling boil. Decrease the heat to medium and simmer for 5 minutes. Strain out the orange zest. Whisk in the softened gelatin mixture until completely dissolved. Slowly stream in the buttermilk mixture, whisking continuously. Pour into 4-ounce ramekins and refrigerate for at least 2 hours, or until fully set and firm.

To make the wine gelée, sprinkle the gelatin over 1/2 cup of the wine in a small bowl and set aside.

Combine the remaining 1 3/4 cups red wine, corn syrup, and sugar in a medium saucepan over medium-high heat. Bring to a boil. Whisk in the softened gelatin mixture. Pour into a half sheet pan and refrigerate for 3 to 4 hours, until completely chilled and set. Cut into 1/4-inch squares. Remove the squares from the sheet pan and reserve for the garnish.

To make the pomegranate sauce, combine the pomegranate juice, sugar, and orange zest in a medium saucepan over high heat. Bring to a rolling boil. Decrease the heat and simmer for 10 minutes. Remove the orange zest Cool completely.

To make the tuiles, combine the butter and confectioners' sugar in a large bowl and cream together until light and fluffy. Slowly add the egg whites, one at a time, beating until well blended, increasing the mixer speed, if necessary. Stop the mixer and add the flour and vanilla. Mix on low speed until just incorporated. Transfer to a bowl, cover with plastic wrap, and let chill in the refrigerator for at

least 1 hour.

Preheat the oven to 325°F. Line a baking sheet with parchment paper.

Spoon the chilled dough into a piping bag fitted with an 8mm round tip. Pipe 4-inch-long cookies onto the prepared baking sheet. Using a spatula, smooth out the dough to make rectangles.

Bake for 3 to 5 minutes, or until the edges are golden brown.

To assemble the dessert, place the chilled panna cotta on serving plates. Pour the pomegranate sauce into a measuring cup with a spout and carefully pour over each panna cotta, covering the surface. Place a tuile on the side of each plate and carefully place some wine gelée cubes on top of the tuiles. Garnish with the mint and serve immediately.

BREAD WINNERS CAFE AND BAKERY
VANILLA CREAM PUFFS WITH FRESH STRAWBERRIES

SERVES 8

VANILLA CUSTARD
2 cups sugar
1/2 cup all-purpose flour
1 teaspoon salt
4 cups whole milk
3 vanilla beans, halved lengthwise
8 large egg yolks
8 teaspoons unsalted butter, cut into small
  pieces

CREAM PUFFS
1 1/2 cups water
1/2 cup unsalted butter
1 1/2 cups all-purpose flour
6 large eggs

GARNISH
12 strawberries, hulled and sliced
Confectioners' sugar

To make the vanilla custard, whisk together the sugar, flour, and salt in a medium bowl and set aside.

Pour the milk into a medium saucepan; scrape in the vanilla seeds and add the pods. Stir together. Cook over medium heat until tiny bubbles begin to form around edges of pan, about 7 minutes. Gradually add the milk mixture to the flour mixture, whisking constantly. Transfer the milk-flour mixture to the saucepan; cook over low heat, whisking constantly, for 5 minutes.

Lightly beat the egg yolks in a small bowl. Pour in a small amount of the hot milk-flour mixture, whisking constantly. Return the mixture to the saucepan. Cook over medium heat, whisking constantly, until the mixture comes to a boil and thickens, 10 to 12 minutes. Remove from the heat; discard the vanilla pods. Whisk in the butter until melted. Pass the custard through a fine-mesh sieve into a medium bowl, forcing it through holes with a rubber spatula. Cover the surface of custard with plastic wrap to prevent a skin from forming. Let stand at room temperature until slightly cooled, about 30 minutes. Refrigerate until set

Preheat the oven to 350°F. Line a baking sheet with parchment paper.

To make the cream puffs, combine the water and butter in a saucepan over high heat and bring to a boil. Add the flour all at once and mix it in with a rubber spatula until it pulls away from the side of the pan and forms a ball. Continue stirring for about 1 minute.

Transfer the dough to an electric mixer fitted with a paddle attachment. Beat on low to medium-low speed until cool. Once there is no heat in the dough, add the eggs, one at a time, until mixed. Spoon the dough into eight equal portions on the prepared baking sheet.

Bake for about 20 minutes, or until a nice brown color. The shell should feel hard and hollow when you pick it up.

Let the puffs set until thoroughly cool.

To assemble the dessert, cut the puffs in half and fill the bottom halves with vanilla custard. Place sliced strawberries on top. Dollop with one more spoonful of custard and then place the remaining halves on top. Dust generously with confectioners' sugar. Serve immediately or refrigerate to serve later.

"Life's uncertain," the slogan here reminds us: "Eat dessert first!" But the many devotees of this quirky Uptown hangout (the original location; there is another in Inwood Village, and a third in Plano) don't need to be reminded. Even when they come for the hearty breakfast and brunch menus and for the New Orleans-esque atmosphere, in this hideaway that rambles around several levels inside and out, dessert always holds sway here.

Bread Winners has attributes beyond its cozy courtyards and rustic ambience, and they are its bakery and catering departments. The bakery turns out fresh breads daily (banana bread is a standout), as well as pastries and other desserts. The list of over one hundred interpretations of pies, cakes, bars, brownies, cheesecakes, and cookies is comprehensive. You'll find apricot cream cheese and cranberry-orange breads; caramel apple, Bourbon pecan, and blackberry pies; and chocolate mousse and banana split tortes, just to name a few options. Patrons with a sweet tooth might even find a certain allure to some of the entrees here: raspberry-chipotle chicken, honey-glazed salmon, and coconut chicken tenders are reminders that it's good to mix flavors.

KENICHI
ASIAN PEAR BREAD PUDDING

SERVES 6 TO 8

1 (16-ounce) package pound cake
1/2 French baguette, about 3/4 pound
2 Asian pears, unpeeled and cut into a
   1/4-inch dice
4 cups heavy cream
1/4 cup firmly packed brown sugar
3 tablespoons minced fresh ginger
1 tablespoon ground cinnamon
1/2 teaspoon ground nutmeg
4 whole eggs

STAR ANISE HONEY
2 cups water
3 star anise pods
1 cup honey

GINGER CRÈME ANGLAISE
3 large egg yolks
2 cups heavy cream
1 tablespoon minced fresh peeled ginger
2 teaspoons granulated sugar

SESAME WHIPPED CREAM
2 cups chilled heavy cream
3 tablespoons confectioners' sugar
1 teaspoon sesame oil

You can tell by the other locations of this trendy Pan-Asian sushi eatery (Austin, Kona and Aspen) that owner Billy Reiger has been deliberate in his selection. In each city, his boutique chain has become a mecca for stylish, hip diners in search of sophisticated food in an equally sophisticated setting. Dallas' Kenichi (named for the co-founder, sushi master Kenichi Kanada) is, by far, the glitziest interpretation.

It's hard to overlook the fiber optic chandeliers—their glowing "tentacles" float above the seating area in the front lounge. They bring to mind—even for those people who've never laid eyes on them—luminescent squids that drift gracefully through ocean waters. The effect is other-worldly, perhaps enhanced by the comprehensive selection of premium sakes (more than 80 varieties).

There is a dynamic here of public versus private: curtain-draped booths provide a quiet setting for sharing multiple courses or attempting the interactive dish, ishiyaki, a sear-it-yourself hot stone for cooking scallops, escolar and beef. But for sheer titillation, patrons love the portholes in the women's lounge that provide a discreet view of the bar below.

Cut the pound cake and baguette into 1/2-inch cubes. Put into a medium mixing bowl.

Combine the Asian pears, cream, brown sugar, ginger, cinnamon, and nutmeg in a medium saucepan over medium heat. Heat until almost to boiling. Remove from the heat and let sit for 15 minutes.

Preheat the oven to 375° F. Butter a 2-inch-deep 9-inch by 13-inch baking pan.

Whisk the eggs in a large bowl until smooth. Slowly add the warm cream mixture, whisking continuously. Add the cream mixture to bread and cake cubes and mix thoroughly. Spoon into the prepared baking pan. Place the bread pudding pan in a slightly larger baking pan and add 1/2 inch warm water to create a water bath.

Cover and bake for 45 minutes. Remove the cover and bake for 10 minutes more. Allow to cool.

To prepare the crème Anglaise, heat the cream in small saucepan almost to a boil. Add the ginger, remove from the heat, and allow to sit for 15 minutes. Strain out the ginger and set aside. Whisk the yolks and sugar in stainless bowl until well blended. Slowly whisk the cream into the yolk mixture. Return to the saucepan and heat on medium-low heat, stirring constantly, until just barely able to smoothly coat the back of a spoon. Cool.

To prepare the star anise honey, combine the water and star anise in a small saucepan and bring to a boil over medium-high heat. Continue to boil until reduced by about 95 percent. Strain out the star anise. Return the reduced liquid to the pan, add the honey, and stir until blended.

To prepare the whipped cream, combine the cream, confectioners' sugar, and sesame oil in a chilled stainless steel bowl. Whisk by hand or beat with an electric mixer until firm peaks form.

To serve, slice the pudding into individual portions. Reheat in microwave for 45 seconds or until warm. Serve warm, drizzled with the crème Anglaise and star anise honey, topped with a dollop of whipped cream.

CHOCOLATE POTS DE CRÈME

SERVES 6 TO 8

CHOCOLATE POTS DE CRÈME
7 large egg yolks
1/2 cup sugar
Pinch of salt
1 teaspoon vanilla extract
2 cups heavy whipping cream
12 ounces Valrhona dark (61 percent cacao)
  chocolate, coarsely chopped
1/4 cup unsalted butter, chilled and diced

PEANUT BRITTLE
1 cup granulated sugar
1 tablespoon corn syrup
2 tablespoons unsalted butter
1/2 cup roasted salted peanuts, chopped

Lightly sweetened whipped cream, to serve

To prepare the pots de crème, beat the yolks with the sugar, salt, and vanilla until pale yellow.

In a saucepan with a heavy bottom, heat the cream until it steams.

Ladle some of the hot cream into the egg mixture, then mix the egg mixture into the rest of the hot cream. Cook over medium heat, stirring constantly with a wooden spoon until the mixture thickens. Remove from the heat and pour the hot mixture into the bowl of a food processor.

With the motor running, gradually add the chocolate, then the butter. When the mixture is smooth, ladle into 8-ounce ramekins, cover with plastic wrap, and chill for at least 2 hours before serving.

Line a sheet pan with a nonstick silicone liner or Silpat.

To prepare the peanut brittle, heat the sugar with the corn syrup and butter in a saucepan with a heavy bottom until it turns a deep golden brown. Stir in the peanuts and pour the mixture onto the prepared sheet pan. Let the brittle cool for 5 to 10 minutes, then break into small pieces.

To serve, garnish each pot de crème with whipped cream and peanut brittle.

Many people in the Baby Boomer generation think of the Kinks' "Lola" as a lover who walked like a man but looked like a woman. But this lovely Lola sends no such mixed messages. Rather, it's an effortlessly elegant, 70-seat restaurant in an old house situated among the galleries that line Fairmount Street. When the weather's pleasant, dining on the front patio will remind travelers of al fresco repasts somewhere in Europe. For owner Van Roberts, who made his fortune in the automobile business, fine cooking is an avocation taken very seriously.

Cuisine could be described as Continental, but reconsidered for the American palate. Sea scallops scented with truffle oil, for instance, come with a side of wild mushroom-sweet potato hash. Roberts simplifies the ordering process with a user-friendly prix fixe menu offering two-, three-, or four-course meals in a small-plate format that gives the diner freedom to pick and choose and chef David Uygur a chance to show off.

Roberts admits to an affinity for desserts, and often returns from his travels to brainstorm. The roasted fresh pineapple drizzled with warm rum sauce he conjured up after a trip to Hawaii is a sweet souvenir for lucky diners.

BLUEBERRY BRIOCHE BREAD PUDDING WITH BOURBON SOUR CREAM SAUCE

SERVES 6 TO 8

BLUEBERRY BREAD PUDDING
1/2 loaf brioche (14 ounces), cut in 1/4-inch
   slices
4 ounces dried blueberries (See Note below)
2 cups half-and-half
2/3 cup granulated sugar
4 large eggs
1 1/2 teaspoons vanilla extract

1 tablespoon unsalted butter, melted
Fresh blueberries, to garnish
Bourbon Sour Cream Sauce
1 cup sour cream
2 tablespoons brown sugar
1 to 2 tablespoons bourbon
1/2 teaspoon vanilla extract

Preheat the oven to 325°F. Brush 1 tablespoon melted butter on the bottom and along the sides of a 9-inch by 13-inch baking dish.

To prepare the bread pudding, trim the crust from the brioche. Set aside. Soak the dried blueberries in hot water to cover until softened, but not mushy. Drain and set aside.

Whisk together the half-and-half, 9 tablespoons of the sugar, the eggs, and vanilla in a medium bowl until smooth. Line the bottom of the prepared baking dish with a layer of sliced brioche. Sprinkle one-third of the blueberries on the bread. Top with one-third of the custard mix. Repeat this process three times, ending with a top layer of bread. Press down lightly to soak the top layer and cover with any remaining custard mix. Cover tightly with foil, but do not allow the foil to touch the pudding. Put the bread pudding pan into the larger pan and add warm water to the larger pan to reach two-thirds of the way up the baking pan.

Bake the pudding for 40 minutes. Carefully remove the foil from the bread pudding and discard. Sprinkle the top of the pudding with the remaining sugar. Bake for 10 minutes more to melt the sugar and create a glaze. Carefully remove the bread pudding pan from the water bath and allow it to cool in the pan.

To prepare the sauce, whisk together the sour cream, brown sugar, 1 tablespoon bourbon, and vanilla until the brown sugar dissolves. Add more bourbon to taste, if desired.

To serve, slice the bread pudding into 3-inch squares and serve warm with fresh berries and a dollop of the bourbon sauce. If you wish to decorate the place with a strawberry sauce, as shown in the photograph at left, see recipe on page 70.

NOTE: You may substitute 1 cup fresh blueberries for the dried blueberries in this recipe; however, dried berries have a much more intense flavor and less water than fresh berries.

Many people have probably whizzed by this former Ramada Inn on their way to the SMU campus or NorthPark Mall and never given the generic building a second look. Now, though, a smart renovation has brought this four-story building into the Mod world. It's been renamed Hotel Lumen for the brightly colored, light-filled windows in front, and for the enlightening experience the Kimpton corporation wants its guests to have while staying. While they were at it, the international hotel chain also snuck in a smart little restaurant, called Social, at the back side of the Lumen.

The hotel's retro feel is reflected in Social's menu, a throwback to a simpler time but with a twist. Perhaps the most universally beloved of all comfort foods—macaroni and cheese—does contain macaroni, as advertised. But the cheese, a gooey blast of melted brie and truffle, elevates the comfort concoction to the level of sophisticated, too. Chef John Schwarzenberger seems to revel in making his patrons take another look at beloved foods they may have taken for granted.

COBBLERS & CRISPS

The cobbler, and especially its kissing cousin, the crisp, is what happens when the concepts behind the pie and the pudding merge. The crisp is, in fact, relatively new on the dessert scene (there's no mention of this fruity alternative in the 1896 Fannie Farmer Cookbook). One British variant, the crumble, made its first appearance during World War II, when rationing severely limited the flour supply. Enterprising Britons made do with leftover bread crumbs for the topping instead of the usual plump biscuit or generous dollop of batter.

Cobblers are very Southern, and for Texans whose dessert philosophy comes straight out of the South, they are just another way to demonstrate enthusiasm for the attributes of the covered fruit pie. Compared to cobblers, pies can actually seem a bit restrained with all their fruit hidden under a crust or peeking out from underneath latticed strips of dough.

The cobbler is packed to overflowing with fruit, and the crust is expected to do double duty: it serves as the topping, but because the fruit filling is poured over the batter too, the dough rises through the fruit and forms a kind of a dumpling after it's baked (that's the gooey part we all love so much). The cobbler is proof that you can never have too much of a good thing.

L'ANCESTRAL
CHERRY CLAFOUTIS

SERVES 10 TO 12

1 cup all-purpose flour
3/4 cup sugar
6 large eggs
Pinch of salt
4 cups milk
2 (15-ounce) cans pitted Bing cherries

Preheat the oven to 500° F. Butter an 8-inch by 12-inch baking dish.

Combine the flour, sugar, eggs, and salt in bowl and mix well. Add the milk and mix until everything is smooth.

Drain the cherries and spread out in the prepared baking dish in an even layer. Pour the batter over the cherries.

Bake for 15 minutes. Decrease the oven temperature to 350°F and continue baking for 1 hour.

Transfer to a rack and cool for about 30 minutes before serving, or let it cool for 3 to 4 hours for a firmer texture.

If you were French and you found yourself in Dallas, you would make a bee-line for this quiet, somewhat rustic favorite of the city's old guard. There are plenty of other French restaurants in town—all exhibit the va-va-voom that is one facet of classical preparation. Here, tout au contraire: It's the old standards at which the chef excels. Soupe a l'oignon, steak tartare, leeks in vinaigrette, escargot in puff pastry, and lamb tenderloin sautéed in mint and cognac are fine examples of French country-style cooking. Simple herbs and vegetables are the stalwarts, and receive respectful treatment from the chef, who has been with the restaurant since it opened in 1983—as has most of the wait staff.

The setting is intimate—just 19 tables, with a few more outside in a small courtyard. Service usually moves at a deliberate pace, which is one way to force harried Americans to slow down and enjoy the fragrant onion tart, sautéed vegetable sides, frites, and especially the spectacular "floating island," the impressive mound of meringue nesting in a pool of crème Anglaise for which the restaurant is deservedly famous.

The celebrated chef and Top Chef lead judge Tom Colicchio came up with the idea for Craft when he developed the New York original: his notion was to mix and match entrees, sides, salads and appetizers so that patrons order exactly what they want, not what someone else thinks they should have.

It also means that Colicchio lavishes attention on every component of the meal: vegetables at Craft are alive with flavor, such as the sweet potato puree vibrant with fresh ginger and spices. Salads here are virtuoso creations. The beet salad is a lesson in four variations of the root—roasted red and yellow beets, pickled chioggias, and two house-made beet chips. Entrees, such as roasted rack of lamb, California squab, and sliced pork tenderloin are robust examples of the chef's finesse with meats. All offerings vary with the seasons, so expect lighter fare in the spring and summer months.

The setting is just as spectacular as the food. The restaurant is tucked into a back corner on the first floor of the W Hotel but seems to have sidestepped the hotel's notorious glitziness. Low booths separated by tubes of fluorescent lights, cowhide paneling, concrete columns, and rows of overhead lighting set the stage for a more substantial kind of glamour.

CRAFT

BLUEBERRY COBBLER WITH LEMON VERBENA FROZEN YOGURT

It is not really important to use blueberries and lemon verbena for these recipes. What is important is using the ripest fruit, grown organically and locally, if possible, that you can find. The recipe works well with plums or peaches in the late summer, rhubarb in the spring, apples or pears in the fall and winter. You will need to adjust the amount of sugar depending upon the sweetness of different fruits, but the biscuit topping and the ratio of ingredients for the yogurt remain the same. Feel free to substitute mint, basil, thyme, rosemary, or any other herb for the lemon verbena. Other great flavor combinations are plums and thyme, peaches and basil, apples and rosemary, and rhubarb and mint.

SERVES 8 TO 12

FROZEN YOGURT
1 ½ cups water
1 1/2 cups fine-grain raw or natural sugar
1/2 teaspoon salt
4 (6-inch) stems lemon verbena
2 cups plain yogurt
2 cups buttermilk

BISCUIT TOPPING
1/2 cup heavy whipping cream, plus more as needed
2 large eggs
5 cups unbleached pastry or cake flour
1 cup fine-grain raw or natural sugar, plus more as needed
1 tablespoon baking powder
1 teaspoon salt
1 Mexican or Tahitian vanilla bean, scraped
3/4 cup unsalted butter, cubed and chilled

FRUIT
12 ounces blueberries
1/4 cup raw sugar
Pinch of ground cardamom
1 teaspoon cornstarch or potato starch
1/2 cup unsalted butter, cubed and chilled

To prepare the frozen yogurt, combine the sugar, salt, and water in a small saucepan over high heat. Bring to a simmer and whisk to dissolve the sugar and salt. Add the lemon verbena, remove from the heat, and allow to steep for at least 30 minutes or up to 1 hour. Strain the syrup into a clean bowl. Add the yogurt and buttermilk, and whisk until smooth. Freeze the yogurt mixture in an ice cream maker according to the manufacturer's directions. Store the frozen yogurt in an airtight container in the freezer until you are ready to serve. It is best eaten within 2 days.

Preheat the oven to 350°F in a conventional oven or 300°F in a convection oven.

To prepare the biscuit topping, whisk together the heavy cream and the eggs in a small bowl and set aside.

Combine the flour, sugar, baking powder, and salt in the bowl of an electric mixer fitted with a paddle attachment. Add the seeds from the vanilla bean and the butter. Mix on medium speed until the butter is well cut in and the mixture resembles coarse meal. Add the heavy cream and egg mixture, and mix just until a sticky dough forms; do not overmix. Pat the dough onto a lightly floured baking sheet or cutting board and cut into 2-inch circles or squares using a pastry cutter or a knife.

To prepare the fruit, toss together the blueberries, sugar, cardamom, and cornstarch in a medium bowl, breaking a few of the berries to allow the sugar and cornstarch to stick to them. Leave most of the berries whole. Add the cold butter piece and toss to mix.

To assemble the dessert, transfer the fruit to a baking dish large enough to hold them. Top the fruit with the biscuits. Brush the tops of the biscuits with heavy cream, and sprinkle them with raw sugar.

Bake the cobbler for about 40 minutes, or until the biscuits are golden brown and the berries are bubbling and slightly thickened. Serve immediately with the frozen yogurt on the side.

COOKIES, CANDIES & SUCH

We've elaborated on the cookie considerably since its humble, and not very sweet, beginnings as a hard little biscuit—and have added to the mix all sorts of delicacies including nuts, fruits, spices, and, of course, chocolate. You could also argue that some cookie ingredients—peanut butter, oatmeal, and ginger, to name just a few—are actually good for you. Or, in the case of ginger, good for what ails you.

Some cookies here in Texas are famous—such as The Zodiac Room's white chocolate cranberry version, or Shinsei's oatmeal cookies. Texas cookies are special to us because they are the perfect agent for showing off what we are really proud of—our ingenuity and certainty that everything that we grow in Texas is the absolute best. The state is famous for pecans—they're luscious and meaty, and combined with the brownie (as in the recipe from Pyramid Restaurant), they make for a hearty confection with a surprisingly robust point of view.

The praline—now a staple in Tex-Mex restaurants—is actually a French delicacy, the mid-17th century invention of Marshal du Plessis-Praslin. Texans have appropriated the sugary confection, but the candy's provenance explains why the recipe here is from St. Germain, one of Dallas' most famous French restaurants. *Naturellement.*

BIJOUX
VALRHONA CHOCOLATE BAR

SERVES 6

PINE NUT CRUST
3 cups all-purpose flour
2 cups pine nuts
1 cup unsalted butter, at room temperature
1/2 cup sugar
1 teaspoon salt
1 large egg, plus 1 large egg yolk

GANACHE
2 1/2 cups heavy cream
1 pound Valrhona Manjari chocolate, coarsely chopped

POACHED SECKEL PEARS
3 cups water
3 cups sweet white wine
1 cup sugar
1 vanilla bean
1 cinnamon stick
3 allspice berries
1 star anise
6 Seckel pears

ROSE ICE CREAM
2 cups milk
2 cups heavy cream
1 cup plus 1 tablespoon sugar
7 large egg yolks
1 teaspoon rose oil
1 teaspoon vanilla extract

STRAWBERRY SAUCE
1 pint fresh strawberries, hulled
1/2 cup sugar, plus more as needed
1/2 teaspoon vanilla extract

PINK PEPPER DUST
1/4 cup pink peppercorns

To make the crust, combine the flour and pine nuts in a food processor and process until the nuts are finely ground.

Cream together the butter and sugar, beating until light and fluffy. Beat in the salt. Beat in the eggs and egg yolk, beating until well blended. Mix in the pine nut mixture. Gather the dough into a ball. Wrap in plastic wrap and chill for 2 hours.

Preheat the oven to 350°F.

On a lightly floured work surface, roll out the dough thickly to fit an 8-inch square baking pan, with the crust coming about 1/4 inch up the sides of the pan.

Bake for 10 to 12 minutes, until golden brown. Let cool on a wire rack.

To make the ganache, bring the cream to a boil in a small saucepan. Remove from the heat and pour over chocolate in a bowl. Let it sit for about 30 seconds. Then whisk together until smooth and pour over the crust. Allow to set up overnight.

To prepare the pears, combine the water, wine, sugar, vanilla bean, cinnamon stick, allspice berries, and star anise in a saucepan. Bring to a boil, then let it cool to room temperature. Peel the pears and submerge them in the liquid, cut a piece of parchment paper to fit the pot, and place it on top. Bring the pears to a simmer. Decrease the heat to keep the liquid just under a simmer, until the pears are about half cooked. If the pears are hard, cook about 25 minutes, if they are medium hard, cook 10 to 15 minutes. (Do not use fully ripe pears.) Turn off the heat and cover with the lid. Let cool to room temperature, then store in the refrigerator in the poaching liquid overnight. Cut the pears in half and remove the core and stem. Return to the liquid until you are ready to serve.

To make the ice cream, combine the milk, cream, and 1/2 cup of the sugar in a saucepan and bring to a boil. Whisk together the egg yolks and the remaining 1/2 cup plus 1 tablespoon sugar. When the milk mixture comes to a boil, slowly pour it into the eggs, whisking constantly. Return the mixture to the saucepan and cook over low heat, stirring constantly until the mixture thickens and coats the back of a spoon. Pass through a fine-mesh strainer to remove any lumps. Stir in the rose oil and vanilla extract and refrigerate overnight. Then freeze in an ice-cream maker according to the manufacturer's directions.

To make the strawberry sauce, combine the strawberries, sugar, and vanilla in a blender and process until smooth. Add more sugar if the berries are a little tart. Strain and chill.

To prepare the peppercorn dust, grind the peppercorns in a spice or coffee grinder. Dry on a paper towel.

To assemble the dessert, slice the chocolate bars into 1 1/2-by 3-inch rectangles, using a heated knife and cleaning it between each cut. Or you can use metal cookie cutters to be more creative with your shapes. The chef has used teardrop-shaped cookie cutters for the bars pictured. Pop the bars out of the pan. Slice the pears and fan out on top of the bars.

To set up each plate, take a spoon and make a line with the strawberry sauce down the center of the plate. Sprinkle a little pink pepper dust on top. Place a chocolate bar on one side of the line and scoop the ice cream on the other.

NOTE: You can chop some nuts to anchor the ice cream. This will keep it from sliding all over the place.

CHOCOLATE SECRETS
My Mother's Favorite Dark Chocolate French Truffles

YIELDS 12 TO 15 TRUFFLES

1 cup heavy cream
2 tablespoons unsalted butter
12 ounces semisweet chocolate chunks,
   chopped uniformly
2 tablespoons cognac
8 ounces best-quality dark chocolate
   (70 percent or more cacao)
Unsweetened cocoa (I like Fauchon and
   Marquise de Sévigné), confectioners' sugar,
   or finely chopped pecans (or use all three),
   for dusting

Combine the cream and butter in a saucepan. Slowly bring to a boil, taking care not to burn the mixture.

Put the semisweet chocolate in a large mixing bowl. Slowly pour the hot cream mixture over the chocolate all at once. Add the cognac and stir until the mixture is smooth. Refrigerate until set, 1 to 2 hours.

Shape the chocolate into small balls using the palms of your hand and then set aside on waxed paper or parchment paper. Return to the refrigerator until chilled.

Melt the dark chocolate in the top of a double boiler set over barely simmering water or in a microwave on a low setting. Remove the chocolate balls from the refrigerator and dip them in melted dark chocolate, and then roll each ball in the cocoa powder, confectioners' sugar, or pecans, or a combination of the three. Return to the refrigerator for about 1 hour.

Note: Melting chocolate can be a little tricky. Chop it into uniform pieces and don't try to melt large bars or blocks. Make sure to avoid any contact with water. Even a few drops of water will cause your chocolate to seize and become lumpy. Slow melting is very important. Chocolate can be temperamental. If you do not take your time, it will not melt smoothly. Stir frequently with a rubber spatula. If you make a mistake, do not worry about it. Just try it again. It's chocolate. It's fun.

When a building has "chocolate" in large capital letters across the front, it's hard to miss the invitation. Inside, the message is borne out with élan--this boutique chocolatier, with its wares arrayed inside a glowing display case in the middle of the store, is what happens when a niche speciality gets all the attention it deserves.

Owner Pam Eudaric-Amiri, a former corporate attorney, is on hand daily to discourse on her favorite topic, chocolate. For customers who like to see everything in print, there is a menu that describes in delicious detail exactly what is offered, with pictures. For example, the notation for the champignon caramel—which not surprisingly looks exactly like a mushroom—reads: "Sweet thick caramel is enhanced with a crunchy croquant and all embodied in dark and white chocolate."

Eudaric-Amiri sells chocolates imported from France, and chocolates handmade in Texas (they are bigger). She insists that chocolate is best enjoyed with red wine, offering a variety of selections and wine tastings for non-believers as well as aficionados. Chocolate Secrets has become something of a date place and neighborhood hang-out, and those looking for a real education like to attend the Thursday night conversational French class.

DRAGONFLY
CRANBERRY ALMOND SHORTBREAD COOKIES

MAKES 3 DOZEN COOKIES

4 large eggs
14 ounces almond paste
1 3/4 cups unsalted butter, at room temperature
1/2 teaspoon baking powder
1/2 teaspoon baking soda
2 tablespoons vanilla paste or vanilla extract
7 1/2 cups bread flour
1/2 cup dried cranberries
1/3 cup sugar

There could hardly be a restaurant with a glitzier pedigree, even in Dallas. Located in the over-the-top Hotel ZaZa, there is no such thing as moderation at Dragonfly (note, for instance, the rooms named "The Last Czar" and "Dangerous Beauty"). The dining room is splashy, awash in rich jewel-tone reds and yellows with Oriental high notes. The Hotel—glittering with chandeliers and wall-to-wall mirrors—promotes itself as a destination for enjoying the high life as well as indulging in a full course of relaxation. Tucked away on a side street in Dallas' current hot neighborhood, Uptown, it's central to everything, yet seductively separate.

The ambience in Dragonfly supports a sense of being away from reality, and the menu is quite intriguing—a thought-provoking mix of Latin, Asian, and Mediterranean influences. Fusion is the goal, but it's achieved in an unselfconscious, even whimsical, manner that encourages diners to experiment and have fun doing so. A word of advice: If something on the menu piques your interest, order it. The menu changes frequently, and what's here today may be gone tomorrow!

Beat together the eggs and almond paste until smooth. Add the butter, baking powder, baking soda, and vanilla and mix well. Slowly incorporate the flour and mix until just combined. Fold the cranberries into the mix.

Form the dough into a log about 2 inches in diameter. Spread the sugar on a work surface and roll the dough log over the sugar. Wrap in plastic wrap and chill until firm, 1 to 2 hours.

Preheat the oven to 350°F.

Slice the dough into rounds about the size of a silver dollar. Place on an ungreased nonstick baking sheet and bake for 10 to 12 minutes, or until the cookies are light brown. Cool them on a wire rack.

FESTIVE KITCHEN
HOLIDAY ICED COOKIES

MAKES 24 COOKIES

COOKIES
3/4 cup unsalted butter
1/2 cup confectioners' sugar
1/2 teaspoon pure Mexican vanilla extract
1 1/3 cups all-purpose flour

ICING
1/2 cup unsalted butter, at room temperature
1/2 cup vegetable shortening
4 cups confectioners' sugar
3 tablespoons meringue powder
5 to 6 tablespoons water
Food coloring

To prepare the cookies, cream the butter in an electric mixer on medium speed. Add the confectioners' sugar and mix until incorporated. Add the vanilla. Blend in the flour. Shape into a flat disk, wrap in plastic wrap, and chill for 30 minutes.

Preheat the oven to 325°F. Line a cookie sheet with parchment paper.

Roll out the dough on a lightly floured board until ¼-inch thick. Cut into shapes. Place on the prepared cookie sheet.

Bake for 11 to 13 minutes, until the cookies are just slightly browned. Cool completely on wire racks before icing.

To prepare the frosting, cream the butter and shortening in an electric mixer on medium speed. Beat in the confectioners' sugar, meringue powder, and almond extract. Add the water a little at a time and continue to beat until there are no lumps and the frosting is a good spreadable consistency. The icing must be very smooth for decorating purposes. Add the food coloring 1 drop at a time until you have the desired color.

Apply the frosting with a palette knife, or pipe it onto the cookie. Allow 20 minutes drying time for the icing.

When a business has an item that's available only during the holiday season, and they sell two-and-a-half tons of it, that item must be something pretty special. That's the fresh cranberry salsa, an exhilarating and a little bit sweet send-up of tried-and-true hot sauce. But this catering company is no stranger to popularity: D Magazine named The Festive Kitchen among its "Best of the Best." The magazine's praise didn't stop with generalities, either. Cookie designer Tracy Dahir might be a genius, and for several years running, the Kitchen's cookie dough has received D's coveted award for "Best Cookie Dough."

The awards accumulate for a reason. Owner Sandy Korem attended Le Cordon Bleu and the Ritz Escoffier cooking schools in Paris. Her executive chef, Raymond Tipps, is also classically trained; both are recipients of the Presidential White House Food Service medallion. Chef Korem enjoys sharing her knowledge and offers hands-on cooking classes. But she also understands that many of her clients don't even have time for classes, much less for cooking. The chef's got a club tailor-made for them—members get meals (and also that famous cookie dough) delivered monthly to their homes. The club is so popular there's a waiting list to join.

PYRAMID RESTAURANT
BITTERSWEET CHOCOLATE AND TEXAS PECAN BROWNIES

SERVES 12

1 1/2 cups unsalted butter
6 ounces bittersweet chocolate, chopped
1 1/2 cups sugar
1 cup unsweetened cocoa powder
1 cup cream cheese, softened
4 large eggs
1 tablespoon vanilla extract
1 cup all-purpose flour
1 cup chopped pecans
1/2 teaspoon salt

ESPRESSO BOURBON MOUSSE
1 1/2 cups whipping cream
3 tablespoons brewed espresso
6 tablespoons unsalted butter
9 ounces bittersweet chocolate, chopped
3 tablespoons Wild Turkey bourbon
3 large eggs

GARNISH
Candied pecans
Chocolate quill

With the skyscrapers of the Central Business District and the new profiles of the Victory Park skyline as its backdrop, the Fairmont Hotel is a happy expression of a Texas truism: Bigger is better. Its restaurant, Pyramid Restaurant, is legendary. Both opened in 1969 and were instantly dubbed luxury destinations in a city fascinated with luxury.

Pyramid has garnered many awards in its day—it's the only restaurant in this part of the state to win AAA's 4-Diamond awards 17 times. Mobil has also bestowed its 4-Star award on the intimate dining establishment. The poshly upholstered room, with wall-to-wall Oriental-style carpeting, cushy chairs, and soft lighting, is an antidote to a harried lifestyle, and Pyramid Restaurant's dress code seems to be a welcome respite from the current trend toward underdressing.

So, too, the food tends toward a refreshing return to the classics: steak au poivre, double lamb chops, and veal chops with crabmeat stuffing represent a style of preparation that's fallen nearly out of fashion. The house signature tortilla soup is a winner at lunch—a more relaxed affair—as are the "killer" fish tacos, Texas smoked brisket, and pecan fingers (ancho-chile breaded chicken with apricot and plum dipping sauce).

Preheat the oven to 325° F. Butter and lightly flour an 8-inch x 8-inch x 2-inch square baking pan.

To prepare the brownies, melt the butter in a small saucepan and bring it to a simmer.

Put the chopped chocolate in a large bowl. Pour in the hot butter and let stand for 40 to 60 seconds. Stir until completely melted. Sift in the sugar and cocoa powder. Beat in the cream cheese, eggs, and vanilla, mixing until smooth. Gently fold in the flour, pecans, and salt. Pour the batter into the prepared baking pan, ensuring it is even.

Bake for 35 to 40 minutes, until a knife inserted near the center comes out clean.

To prepare the mousse, combine the cream, espresso, and butter in a small saucepan over medium heat and heat until the cream is scalded.

Put the chopped chocolate in a large mixing bowl. Pour the hot cream mixture over the chocolate and stir until the chocolate is melted and the mixture is smooth. Whisk in the eggs and rum until smooth. Cover with plastic wrap and refrigerate for 35 to 40 minutes.

To assemble, top the warm brownie with a dollop of the espresso bourbon mousse, and garnish with candied pecans and, if desired, a chocolate quill (any good commercial variety will do).

SHINSEI
LYNAE'S FAMOUS OATMEAL COOKIES

MAKES 4 DOZEN

1 cup vegetable shortening (Crisco is recommended)
1 cup firmly packed brown sugar
1 cup granulated sugar
2 whole large eggs
1 teaspoon vanilla extract
3 cups old-fashioned rolled oats
1 1/2 cups all-purpose flour
1 teaspoon baking soda
1 teaspoon salt

Preheat oven to 350°F. Spray cookie sheets with nonstick cooking spray.

Combine the shortening, brown sugar, granulated sugar, eggs, and vanilla in a food processor and process until blended. Mix the oats, flour, baking soda, and salt in a large bowl. Add the shortening mixture and stir until well blended.

Spoon the cookie dough, using 1 tablespoon per cookie, onto the prepared cookie sheets, 1 to 1½ inches apart.

Bake for 20 minutes, until golden, rotating the sheets halfway through for even baking. Transfer to wire racks to cool completely.

The facts that the sous chef Shuji Sugawara has sideburns and a bouffant hairstyle reminiscent of Elvis', or that executive chef Casey Thompson was in the cast of the reality television show "Top Chef," or even that the husbands of the two owners—Lynae Fearing and Tracy Rathbun—are celebrated chefs themselves only add to the mystique of this pan-Asian kitchen.

Chef Thompson oversees a menu that rises to the duality that is the essence of Asian cooking. She has developed items that are both daring and subtle, such as a suave rendition of miso-broiled black cod, and nuanced sushi that's smooth and addicting.

Desserts are usually not the focus of Asian dining, but at Shinsei the offerings suggest traditional flavors (such as the cinnamon chocolate cake with green tea ice cream or the tempura banana split). A favorite, though, are the distinctly American oatmeal cookies—the essence of simplicity that's an achievement with a lot of mystique. And, mystique is actually part of the deal here: interior designer Greg O'Neal has created a moody space that manages to exude both an energetic vibe and Zen sensibility.

ST. GERMAIN
CREAMY PRALINES

MAKES 2 DOZEN

1 cup granulated sugar
1 cup firmly packed light brown sugar
3/4 cup unsalted butter
1/2 cup light corn syrup
1 (14-ounce) can sweetened condensed milk
1/8 teaspoon salt
1 teaspoon vanilla extract
3 cups pecan pieces

Grease a sheet of waxed paper. Place on a flat surface or sheet pan and set aside.

Combine the granulated sugar, brown sugar, butter, corn syrup, condensed milk, and salt in a tall, heavy saucepan over low heat. Cook, stirring gently and scraping the bottom and sides of the pan, until the butter melts. Increase the heat to medium-high and continue cooking, stirring frequently, until the mixture reaches 238° to 245°F on a candy thermometer, about 10 minutes.

Remove the pan from the heat and stir in the vanilla and pecans. Continue stirring until the mixture becomes thick and holds a shape when dropped onto the waxed paper. Working rapidly, set the pan on a folded dish towel and begin scooping the soft praline with one metal spoon while scraping the mixture off with the second spoon onto the waxed paper. Let stand until firm, up to 2 hours.

Oooh, la la! Frommer's congratulates this tiny, ultra-French restaurant for being "capable of making Dallas feel like Paris, and that's saying something!" It's true that the St. Germain—and the boutique hotel of the same name where it's located—are truly oblivious to this big, bustling city. And that's the charm—New Orleans and 19th-century France are the predominant influences, much to the delight of patrons.

The romantic restaurant is intimate—just seven tables in the dining room that overlooks an ivy-covered French Quarter-style garden courtyard. "One of America's top restaurants," affirms the 2006 Zagat Survey of Restaurants.

The menu for the multi-course prix fixe dinners change regularly, but favorites are always the cunning disc of seared foie gras on crisp cinnamon bread and the roasted sea bass resting on fried eggplant. Guests will have time to prepare themselves for what's ahead—you must order your entrée 24 hours in advance. Champagne bar service is a popular option for concert-goers before a show. Foie gras, oysters Rockefeller and assorted canapés make a light dinner; afterward, a chocolate dessert trio and coffee keep night owls alert.

White Chocolate Cranberry Cookies

MAKES 2 DOZEN

1/2 cup unsalted butter, softened
1 cup firmly packed light brown sugar
1 cup granulated sugar
2 large eggs
1 teaspoon almond extract
2 cups all-purpose flour
1 teaspoon salt
1/4 teaspoon baking powder
1 cup toasted sliced almonds
3/4 cup sun-dried cranberries
1 1/2 cups white chocolate chips or morsels

Preheat the oven to 300°F. Grease a large cookie sheet.

Cream the butter with the brown and granulated sugars with an electric mixer until fluffy. Add the eggs and almond extract and beat on low speed until well combined.

Sift the flour, salt, and baking powder in a mixing bowl. Beat into the butter mixture on low speed, stopping the mixer once to scrape down the sides. Stir in almonds, cranberries, and white chocolate chips. Drop by large tablespoons or a 1-ounce scoop onto the prepared cookie sheet 2 inches apart. Flatten slightly.

Bake for 20 minutes, until golden. Cool on wire racks.

As the Dallas Morning News has noted, "If there's a semi-sacred rite of culinary passage for Dallas gourmets, it may be this: going to the downtown Neiman Marcus for lunch at the Zodiac…." Located on the sixth floor of the original Neiman's, the Zodiac is now over 50 years old, but showing no signs of age. In fact, the multi-tiered restaurant is snazzier than ever, a gracious space with a yellow wall so vibrant the color alone could re-energize flagging shoppers.

The most famous item on the menu, presented to diners the moment they arrive, is the off-the-menu popover—a light-as-air concoction that's even better when slathered with the Zodiac Room's signature strawberry butter. Diners know, though, to leave room for the chef's special, a seasonal offering that changes daily. Perhaps the all-time favorite dish is the orange soufflé, which is always on the menu.

One of the many pleasures of the Zodiac Room experience is the service, which deftly toes the line between genteel and stuffy. The staff is unfailingly charming, and under their ministrations the temptation is strong (but never strong enough) just to remain in your chair for the rest of the afternoon.

ICE CREAM & SAUCES

Ice cream may be the one dessert that is required to meet federal nutritional guidelines (it must contain a minimum of 10 percent milk fat and 20 percent total milk solids)—that's how serious we are about how it should taste. Texans are especially devoted to ice cream, so it should come as no surprise that their state is home to the largest franchisee for the global ice cream and fast food restaurant, Dairy Queen.

Why do Texans love their ice cream so passionately? Maybe it's because summers are long and hot and ice cream is the ideal antidote to the doldrums. Likely, too, it's because ice cream is universally associated with a "party." No birthday party would be complete without it.

For that matter, many desserts would be incomplete without it, too. Ice cream is an all-purpose add-on. Pies, cakes, cobblers, crisps, cookies, and candies all taste better alongside or beneath a big scoop of the creamy frozen confection. And, even if ice cream begins to melt on that slice of hot pie, it's instantly transformed from a side dish to a dreamy sauce, providing that special something to make your dessert better than ever.

2900
GODIVA CHOCOLATE BOMBE

SERVES 6

6 (1-ounce) squares dark chocolate, plus 3 (1-ounce) squares dark chocolate, cut in half
3 (1-ounce) squares semisweet chocolate
1/2 cup unsalted butter, softened
3/4 cup all-purpose flour
1 1/2 cups confectioners' sugar
3 large whole eggs plus 4 large egg yolks

1 teaspoon vanilla extract
Seeds from 1 vanilla bean
3 tablespoons Godiva Original Chocolate Liqueur
Ice cream, to serve
Whipped cream, to serve
Caramel and chocolate sauce, to serve

Preheat the oven to 425°F. Grease the insides of six custard cups or a six-hole muffin tin.

Melt the six 1-ounce squares of dark chocolate with the semisweet chocolate in the top of a double boiler over barely simmering water. Add the flour and confectioners' sugar. Stir in the eggs and egg yolks until smooth. Stir in vanilla extract, vanilla seeds, and chocolate liqueur. Divide evenly among the six cups.

Bake for 16 minutes, until the edges are firm but the center is still gooey.

To serve, run a knife along edges of the cups to loosen the bombes and place each on a plate. Push one of the remaining 1/2-ounce pieces of chocolate into center of each. Top with ice cream (we have used peppermint, Macadamia nut, vanilla, and strawberry), whipped cream, and a drizzle of sauce.

"Modern soul food" is the draw at this intimate dining room adjacent to its sister (and more-casual) restaurant, Thomas Avenue Beverage Company. It's the brainchild of chef Mike Smith, former executive chef at the Beverage Company. The culinary pioneer saw a niche for upscale reinterpretation of food with soul and established 2900 as a place he could wield his magic on standards such as beef tenderloin. (Smith's version is stuffed with Manchego and served with a mound of sassy chorizo cheese grits and cilantro cream sauce.)

Drama matters here, and it applies to the menu offerings and the setting. Romantically moody lighting—there's enough to see the bold prints of European liqueur ads on the walls—focuses attention on the food. Even the black-clad servers seem to disappear discreetly into the shadows. For those in need of diversion, there's always the brightly lit kitchen—within view just beyond the glass wall—where Smith and his team busy themselves. Besides the standard choices, Smith features two entrée specials nightly, plus an appetizer, a soup, and a dessert. Wine dinners are special treats, often highlighting wines debuting in Texas.

TAHITIAN VANILLA BEAN FRENCH TOAST

SERVES 4

RUM-CARAMEL SAUCE
1 cup granulated sugar
Water
1/2 cup heavy cream
1/4 cup rum
1/4 cup chopped pecan halves

FRENCH TOAST AND BANANAS
3/4 cup granulated sugar
4 large eggs
2 cups milk

1 vanilla bean, split lengthwise and scraped
4 slices brioche, cut 1-inch thick
1/2 cup unsalted butter
2 bananas, sliced

ASSEMBLY
Ice cream
1/4 cup chopped crystallized ginger
Confectioners' sugar
Fresh mint leaves

To make the sauce, combine the sugar with enough water to dissolve the sugar in a medium-size saucepan over high heat. Cook until the sugar is completely dissolved and begins to turn golden brown. Slowly add the heavy cream; the mixture will boil up and overflow the pot if you do not add it slowly. Stir in the rum and chopped pecans. Reserve and keep warm.

To prepare the French toast, combine ½ cup sugar, eggs, and milk in a medium-size mixing bowl. Mix until well combined. Add the seeds from the vanilla bean and mix until well combined. Place the sliced brioche in the milk mixture and let soak for about 3 minutes, until the milk mixture is soaked into bread.

Preheat the oven to 250° F.

Melt 1/4 cup butter in a large sauté pan over medium heat. Add 2 slices of the soaked brioche. Cook on both sides until golden brown and cooked through. Keep warm in the warm oven. Repeat with the remaining butter and brioche.

To prepare the caramelized bananas, slice the bananas lengthwise and remove the peel. Sprinkle the bananas with the remaining ¼ cup sugar. With a blowtorch, caramelize the sugar until golden brown.

To assemble, place a piece of French toast in the center of each of four large round plates. Cover the French toast with the rum-caramel sauce. Place a caramelized banana on top of the sauce on each serving. Place a scoop of your favorite ice cream on top. Garnish with crystallized ginger, confectioners' sugar, and mint.

You'd be correct in thinking that the name alludes to owner Michael Bratcher's novel Tex-Asian concept—a fusion of culinary ideas that has electrified the local food scene. But also, this downtown hot spot is located in the historic Dallas Power and Light building, which has been sleekly renovated in an industrial-meets-Asian vein—and which also has powered many a local fuse. Now, the spark for this 75-seat restaurant comes from a rooftop bar, blue lights, palm trees, and bamboo water garden. And also the food.

Chef Blaine Staniford's quirky pairing of Texas tastes with traditional Asian is a stroke of genius: tenderloin of beef packs a punch courtesy of chipotle butter and a side of Japanese eggplant; a hearts of Romaine "taco" comes loaded with spiced chicken, Mandarin oranges, and a miso-Caesar dressing. Fuse is popular for cocktails before dinner, too; and a cigar bar provides new ways to savor an evening out on the town. Located across the street from the flagship Neiman Marcus, this cool place is right in the middle of all kinds of action.

GEORGE CATERING
White Chocolate Peach Parfait

SERVES 4

3 ounces fresh ginger
10 ounces white chocolate
2 large eggs
1 1/2 cups heavy cream
4 ripe peaches
1/2 cup firmly packed brown sugar
Mint leaves, to garnish
Crystallized ginger, to garnish

The Park Cities events not catered by George are few and far between. Chef George Brown and his wife, Chef Katie Brown, have more than 23 years of experience in the food industry—and their promise as culinary stars was obvious from the start. Food & Wine *magazine named them one of the country's top ten new chefs in 1997.*

George's motto, "Food is life," is an indication of how serious the two chefs are about food—the couple specializes in modern American cuisine made with seasonal ingredients. Favorites such as pork stew with poblanos, tomatillos, corn, and lime or chipotle-rubbed beef tenderloin with charred tomato sauce and avocado pico de gallo are zesty examples of the magic fresh herbs and vegetables can work on seemingly ordinary dishes.

No party is complete without a sweet send-off, and the husband-and-wife team has concocted memorable options. Homemade milkshakes like you've never had before (liquor optional), cheesecake lollipops dipped in chocolate, and warm dried-cranberry tart with vanilla Bourbon sauce have the double advantage of being delicious but also lots of fun to consume.

Grate the ginger and wrap in a piece of cheesecloth. Squeeze the juice out. You should have 3 tablespoons. Set aside.

Melt the white chocolate in the top of a double boiler over barely simmering water. Stir in the eggs with a whisk. Stir in the ginger juice. Whip the cream to soft peaks and fold into the white chocolate and refrigerate.

Place the peaches in a pot of just boiling water for 1 minute. Remove from the water and peel off the skin. Cut into a medium dice. Toss the diced peaches with the brown sugar and let macerate for 30 minutes.

Layer the peaches with the white chocolate mousse in four 8-ounce glasses. Garnish with mint and crystallized ginger.

INDEX

My sweet tooth is well documented, and where it came from isn't much of a mystery. My late father— a finicky, sometimes unenthusiastic eater—always perked up at the sight of a good dessert. Our preferences, too, were conveniently complementary. He liked cake but disdained the icing; cake's OK by me but I LOVE icing. We worked well as a team when it came to finishing off a hefty hunk of moist cake topped with creamy drifts of frosting—and nothing went to waste.

My mother excelled in certain culinary areas like soups and salad dressing, but especially brownies and meringue pies. I am sure that my childhood was enriched in more ways than one by her virtuosity with a few basic ingredients (and no mixes!).

Now, my husband Charles Lohrmann has taken over the helm and is a clever and concerned guide when it comes to searching out worthwhile desserts. He is well aware that occasionally my tastes descend to embarrassing depths, and he will supply me with a few Chunkys to see me through those episodes. But, Charles' natural exuberance is also the reason I am not ashamed to order multiple desserts at a single sitting—he knows, perhaps better than I do, that a real meal is never complete unless a diner acknowledges a chef's achievements from the beginning of the menu to the very (and never bitter) end.

I owe a debt of gratitude to other people who contributed in more immediate ways. Janice Shay was kind enough to ask me to write Dallas Classic Desserts, *and then obliged me with a beautifully designed book. Photographer Robert Peacock's delicious photographs make me want to give up entrees and appetizers forever. And, thanks to the diligence of the editorial team, I'm confident that we've given you, the reader, reliable facts—and that's what matters to anyone who cooks.* —H.T.